ONE~WAY CHOICES in a WRONG~WAY World

Growing the Fruit of Righteousness

Danny Pelfrey

ACCENT BOOKS
Denver, Colorado

ACCENT BOOKS
A division of Accent Publications
12100 West Sixth Avenue
P.O. Box 15337
Denver, Colorado 80215

Copyright © 1991 Accent Publications
Printed in the United States of America

ISBN 0-89636-273-6
Library of Congress Catalog Card Number 90-85183

Dedicated
to
Wanda, Kellie, and Sandy

Their influence and encouragement is vital to my
ability to be useful.

CONTENTS

Introduction

While in southwest Illinois to speak for a series of special meetings, I asked my host, a successful farmer, "Tom, what would you say is the secret to productive farming?"

Without hesitation, Tom answered confidently, "There is no secret. Every farmer knows that successful farming is the result of a series of right choices." He went on to explain that growing good crops is the natural result of choosing the right ground, the right timing, the right fertilizer, the right seed, the right help, the right equipment, etc. He then qualified his observations with this statement, "But even when you make all the right decisions, it is still in God's hands."

I would say that the highest productivity level in Christian living is also attained by making a series of right choices. The content of this book is geared to help us make those choices which enable us to put our lives in God's hands for maximum results.

Paul wrote to the Philippians about his aspirations for them: "And this is my prayer: that your love may abound more and more in knowledge and depth of insight, so that you may be able to discern what is best and may be pure and blameless until the day of Christ, filled with the fruit of righteousness that comes through Jesus Christ—to the glory and praise of God" (1:9-11).

This is the goal of every committed Christian: to live a life and engage in the activities that will bring glory and praise to God. The measure of a Christian's life is the quality and quantity of that righteous fruit it produces.

We know that luck has nothing to do with what we accomplish. It is choosing God's way, obeying Him, and pursuing that way until it becomes part of our essential life crop that enables us to attain the best in life.

It is my prayer that this book will give you the help you need to travel with the greatest degree of effectiveness through that fantastic adventure we call life. May every day of your life be filled with the fruit of righteousness that comes through Jesus—to the glory and praise of God.

chapter one

Choose the Right Direction

"I'm not pleased with the direction in which my life is going," my troubled friend informed me.

I needed more information if I was to help him. I nudged, "Tell me where you see your life going."

He answered, "Right now it is going nowhere." After a brief pause, he corrected himself. "No, that is not true. I am not sitting still. I am moving backwards."

God allows us to choose our direction, to move forward, backward, or just sit in neutral. However, forward is the only way to satisfaction, excitement, purpose, and most importantly, fruitfulness. My friend's realization about the direction in which he was headed proved to be a pivotal point in his life. Today, having reversed his direction, his life is full of wonderful fruit.

What direction is your life going?

God made sure of our ability to shift into forward, neutral, or reverse when He instilled in us freedom of choice. Our challenge is to move in that direction which will bring to our lives the satisfaction, excitement, purpose, and fruitfulness we—and *He*—desire.

The writer of Hebrews compared life to running a race. He said, "Let us run with patience the race that is set before us" (12:1, KJV). People running in a race move forward toward the finish line. I have never seen a race in which the participants ran backward.

"Full steam ahead" is the cry of those who make a difference in our world.

Spiritual progress enables Christians to move on to greater achievement and, at the same time, it qualifies us for greater blessings. The Bible leaves no doubt the Lord is pleased most when we choose spiritual growth. Without question, God's way is forward (Philippians 3:13-14).

The Old Testament Illustrates It

The children of Israel were reluctant at first to follow Moses out of Egypt. However, God gave Moses some signs for the benefit of the Pharaoh which must have impressed them, too, because they consented to follow. Everything seemed to be fine—until Pharaoh's army moved in on them from the rear.

The Israelites began to grumble and murmur. They said to Moses, "Was it because there were no graves in Egypt that you brought us to the desert to die? What have you done to us by bringing us out of Egypt? Didn't we say to you in Egypt, 'Leave us alone; let us serve the Egyptians?' It would have been better for us to serve the Egyptians than to die in the desert!" (Exodus 14:11-12).

They were laborers, not soldiers. They knew that a battle with the large, well trained Egyptian army would be suicide.

Moses did the right thing. He went to God for help.

God responded to Moses with crystal clear instructions: "Why are you crying out to me? Tell the Israelites to move on" (Exodus 14:15).

How could they go forward when the Red Sea was in front of them?

God told Moses, "Raise your staff and stretch out your hand over the sea to divide the water so that the Israelites can go through the sea on dry ground" (Exodus 14:16).

Moses convinced the people to follow God's instructions. God miraculously saved them and, in the process, destroyed Pharaoh's army.

The lesson for them and us is clear. God instructed them to go forward. They obeyed; God removed the obstacle.

The New Testament Teaches It

In I Peter 2:2 Peter wrote, "Like newborn babies, crave pure spiritual milk, so that by it you may grow up in your salvation."

Undeveloped skills limit a baby's ability to perform. These words remind us that we come into the Lord with some growing to do as spiritual babies, and we, too have undeveloped skills that limit our effectiveness for the Lord.

Parents take care of their newborn baby because the baby cannot meet his own basic needs. I have never heard a parent suggest to a newborn baby, "If you need a dry diaper, you will find it in the dresser drawer." We do not expect a baby to prepare meals or drive to the doctor to keep an appointment. However, as the infant grows to adolescence and then adulthood, he assumes full responsibility for himself.

Likewise, newborn spiritual babies are dependent on more mature members of the spiritual family. However, with growth and nurturing, they gain new strength, becoming less dependent on other Christians and more capable of a productive Christian life.

In I Corinthians 3:1-4 Paul wrote to the Corinthian Christians a rather serious accusation.

> Brothers, I could not address you as spiritual but as worldly—mere infants in Christ. I gave you milk, not solid food, for you were not yet ready for it. Indeed, you are still not ready. You are still worldly. For since there is jealousy and quarreling among you, are you not worldly? Are you not acting like mere man? For when one says, "I follow Paul," and another, "I follow Apollos," are you not mere man?

It is natural for immature children to cry, fight, and fuss. Evidently, many Christians at Corinth were immature. They fought among themselves. They refused to deal with such problems as immorality in their ranks. They abused the Lord's Supper, spiritual gifts, and much more. Frankly, the church in that city was "a mess."

They were guilty of spiritual stagnation. The result was that the church in Corinth did not function as God intended. Paul wrote his first letter to the Corinthians primarily as a plea for the Christians there to grow up. They needed to move beyond the place where they had settled in their spiritual development.

Growth is natural. Stagnation is unnatural.

Kellie, my oldest daughter, weighed six pounds at birth, but we weren't worried. We would have panicked, though,

if she had remained at six pounds a year later. That little
girl who weighed six pounds at birth is now a young adult.
It has been exciting for us as her earthly parents to watch
her grow in size, skill, and understanding.

Can you imagine how much more exciting it must be
for the Father to watch the progress in His children, too?

While visiting in a children's hospital, I had an unfor-
gettable experience. A friend introduced me to parents of
a patient, a baby boy, several months old. I noticed the
child was smaller than most infants are even at birth. I
later remarked to my friend, "That baby surely seems to
be small."

He explained, "Yes, that is the reason he is here. He
has not increased in size since birth. A rare affliction will
prevent him from growing any larger. They do not expect
him to live much longer."

A tragedy and a heartache for the parents. But do we
grieve the heart of our heavenly Father when we refuse
to grow?

Spiritual infancy is something each of us can change.
Christians do not have to be "babies" all their lives. By
exerting the appropriate effort we can grow strong in the
Word and in our faith. God wants the best for His children.
He wants us to grow into happy, useful, mature members
of His family. He wants us to choose a pattern of forward
progress.

Paul Demonstrated It

Paul wrote to the Philippians:

> Not that I have already obtained all this, or have
> already been made perfect, but I press on to take
> hold of that for which Christ Jesus took hold of

me. Brothers, I do not consider myself yet to have
taken hold of it. But one thing I do: Forgetting
what is behind and straining toward what is ahead,
I press on toward the goal to win the prize for
which God has called me heavenward in Christ
Jesus (3:12-14).

This singleminded statement of purpose reveals three important principles vital to our emerging usefulness to Christ.

(1) *Paul proclaimed that he would not allow anything to distract him from his quest.* He wrote, "I press on toward the goal to win the prize..." (v. 14).

Paul moved forward. Growth was a way of life for him. He refused to allow Satan or the world or his circumstances to distract him. He set his sights heavenward, refusing to stray from the direction in which he was focused.

I learned an important lesson as a high school runner. The runner who looks back or even glances to his right or left is likely to lose time. I recall a teammate losing a victory in the one-hundred-yard dash because he failed to keep his focus on the finish line. To win, we must focus on the goal, refusing to be distracted from our forward progress.

(2) *Paul announced dissatisfaction with the level he had already attained.* He said, "not that I have already obtained this, or have already been made perfect" (v. 12). He also stated, "I do not consider myself yet to have taken hold of it" (v. 13).

If ever a man could be justified in being comfortable with his spiritual status, Paul could. He was a giant in the first century church. His influence for the Lord was widely felt. He no doubt led hundreds of people to know the Lord Jesus Christ as Savior. His efforts contributed to the growth of the church. He sacrificed freely for the cause of Christ, but Paul refused to be satisfied. There was more he could do; there was a greater depth of spirituality than he had already attained. He would keep on, moving closer and closer to the Lord.

The problem with becoming satisfied in our Christian lives is the tendency to stop on that plateau where we are comfortable when the Lord has so much more for us. A wise friend advised me, "Don't ever stop growing, because you will always be short of your potential as long as you live in this world."

A high school basketball coach told me, "Now that my team has won the sectional, I have my work cut out for me." He went on to explain, "The boys consider their season a success. They are satisfied with what they have accomplished, but they have the potential to go much farther."

We trust the doctor who is never satisfied with his medical knowledge. The best educators are the teachers who are never satisfied with their current knowledge. It is growing people who are most useful to their fellow man. It is growing Christians who are most useful to God and His church.

(3) *Paul also made it clear he would not be slowed down by failures he had experienced.* He said, "…Forgetting what is behind…" (v. 13). Obviously, Paul did not dwell too much on his past victories so as not to become satisfied. But perhaps even more important, he did not dwell on his defeats. That would surely discourage him! Paul undoubtedly had some failures, but he refused to be discouraged by them.

Failure can be a great teacher, though. It has been said that "Failure is the springboard to success." Many of the greatest successes in history have come only after a large number of failures. It is advisable to remember failure—but only for reference in future attempts, as building blocks that show you what won't work so you can concentrate on what does.

Surely the life, ministry, and teachings of Paul clearly demonstrate that God's way is "forward."

The First Church Practiced It

In Acts 2:41 Luke tells us the Lord added three thousand people to the church on the very first day of its existence. Verse 42 provides a report on the actions of those people after they became part of the body of Christ. "They devoted themselves to the apostles' teaching and to the fellowship, to the breaking of bread and to prayer."

That verse reveals the four-part formula of the early church which empowered its members to move forward in the right direction. Bible study plus fellowship plus witnessing plus worship plus prayer equals spiritual progress.

We see evidence of this progress all through verses 43-47. Those first-century Christians took care of the needs of their brothers and sisters. They were united. They worshiped God on a regular basis. They were glad and sincere. The Lord added to the church daily. Something special was happening in the lives of those people. They were not the same people they had been when they first heard Peter preach on the day of Pentecost.

A survey of the book of Acts reveals that the early Christians did not plateau. The church prospered. Multitudes enlisted their lives for the cause of Christ. They zealously took the gospel with them when scattered by persecution. They became a people "on fire" for their Lord.

Several years ago, Dr. W. A. Criswell stated, "With the present trend, by the year 2000 less than two percent of the human population will be identified with evangelical Christianity."

That is a sobering prognosis for those of us who love the Lord! How can the trend be reversed? The answer seems to be the development of strong, knowledgeable Christians. Churches would do well to see themselves as "boot camps" equipping Christian soldiers capable of turning the battle.

The good news is that we can turn things around through personal growth in our relationship with the Lord. The trend can be reversed when Christians take seriously God's principles for Christian living and maturity. Hope for the future of the church lies with those who have a desire to do better than their best—those who will go beyond self.

Is that possible? The answer is "yes." It happens when we allow the Lord to control our lives. We can go beyond ourselves because God's Holy Spirit dwells in us. Through Him, we can be more than we are in the flesh.

Several years ago a young Christian visited my office. With head bowed he said to me, "I'm not satisfied with my meager attempts at service for the Lord. I want to be better and I want to do more. Will you help me?"

What a question!

It is people like that young man who will make a difference—people who chose to go forward. It is people who have decided they will pay the price for growth who will grow the fruit of righteousness to record-breaking sizes in their lives.

While looking at suits in a department store one day, I spotted a beautiful one on the racks. I decided, "That's the one for me." The size was just right! Then I looked at the price tag and was somewhat stunned. I quickly rationalized, "That suit is not as nice as I thought it was. The one on the other rack ($100.00 less expensive) is far more desirable." But actually, it was the cost that scared me away.

Too many of us today focus on the cost of following Jesus. And there is, indeed, a cost involved in "pressing forward." Let us not be frightened away by the cost. The end result justifies a thousand times over the cost of getting there. Our effort to move forward is an investment that will reap benefits now and in eternity.

PRINCIPLES TO PONDER:

1. God's way is forward.

2. We can expect God to deal effectively with our obstacles when we choose His way.

3. Spiritual maturity is attained only by working at it.

4. Growth is natural; stagnation is unnatural.

5. First-century Christians attained spiritual growth by diligent Bible study, fellowship, worship, and prayer.

6. We can expect spiritual growth to cost something.

PRACTICING THE PRINCIPLES:

1. Ask a growing Christian who has known you for some time to evaluate honestly your spiritual growth.

2. Spend some time discussing with family members or friends the possibility of sharing in activities that will help to produce spiritual growth. Get involved in at least one such activity.

3. Using a concordance to find every New Testament passage containing the word "grow," read each passage, making notes on how it is used and/or the conditions for growth.

chapter two

Choose the Right Goals

"What do you want to do with your life?" I asked.

"I have never felt it important for me to decide that. I just let it happen," the young man replied.

That is one approach to life, but certainly not the one that will produce the choicest fruit. It may be a cliche, but, nevertheless, it is true: "He who aims at nothing will hit it." We accomplish the most when we set specific goals and make definite plans that will enable us to reach them.

Those principles are the same for growing spiritually.

We cannot expect to have a significant impact on the world or our neighborhoods if we choose to go through life like a toy train speeding round and round the track headed nowhere. Another danger is that we will make our goals so broad that they cease to be of any real value.

A salesman passing through a small community noticed several targets on the side of a barn. He was amazed that an arrow was right in the center of each bull's-eye. He went into a small general store nearby where several men were standing around.

"Someone in this community must be quite a marksman," the salesman commented after telling them about the arrows in the center of the targets.

"I don't know about that," an old gentleman answered with a drawl, "but we do have a fellow who likes to shoot arrows into the side of a barn and then paint targets around them."

It isn't difficult to hit targets as broad as the side of a barn, but what do we accomplish unless the goals are specific?

In I Corinthians 10:23 through 11:1, Paul wrote about the freedom we have in the Lord. He set the stage for some guiding principles with this statement, "Everything is permissible—but not everything is beneficial." Paul reminds us that God gave us freedom of choice; however, not every direction open to us is good. He goes on from there to suggest some considerations for exercising the freedom God has given us. These principles give us guidelines for setting goals that will enable us to have the greatest influence for Christ.

Set Constructive Goals

The first principle for goal setting is that Christians should set constructive goals.

The Guinness Book of Records is full of information about people setting records, but some of those accomplishments contributed absolutely nothing to the good of anyone. But what does it matter that a particular person ate more of a particular kind of food than everyone else? God calls us to set goals that will enable us to make a difference.

A teenage boy with some interest in mechanical things rebuilt a small engine. He invested many hours of labor, and the motor ran like a top. He was proud of his work. He invited a friend into the garage to examine his handiwork. He started the engine and excitedly asked, "Isn't that a beautiful sound? She purrs lik a kitten!"

"Yes," replied his friend, "but what does it do? It doesn't turn any wheels; it doesn't produce any electricity. It just sits there and uses gasoline."

God did not intend for our lives to be like that motor. Life is more than just using up energy. Every life has the potential to be fruitful.

But not only are some goals not constructive, they may be destructive. Jesus asked, "What good is it for a man to gain the whole world, yet forfeit his soul?" (Mark 8:36).

Jesus offered a simple warning in His Sermon on the Mount, "Do not store up for yourselves treasures on earth, where moth and rust destroy, and where thieves break in and steal. But store up for yourselves treasures in heaven, where moth and rust do not destroy, and where thieves do not break in and steal. For where your treasure is, there your heart will be also" (Matthew 6:19-21).

We would do well to evaluate our goals regularly. We might ask ourselves questions like: "Even if I accomplish my present goals, will it make any difference to anyone?" Another appropriate question: "Are my present goals distracting me from what is really important?" Constructive goals are necessary for growing the fruit of righteousness.

Set Goals That Will Trigger Blessings For Others

The second principle for goal setting is that Christians should set goals that will enable them to bless others.

Paul wrote, "Nobody should seek his own good, but the good of others" (I Corinthians 10:24).

Paul continues to emphasize this principle in verses 25–30 of I Corinthians 10. There he deals with the question of eating meat offered to idols. His conclusion is that eating such meat is not necessarily a sin, however it can be, if your action causes someone else to stumble. Paul makes it extremely clear that our freedom must sometimes be sacrificed for the sake of others.

Paul wrote, "...I try to please everybody in every way. For I am not seeking my own good, but the good of many, so that they may be saved" (v. 33).

Life is most productive when we approach it with sensitivity toward the needs of our friends, family, neighbors, co-workers, strangers. People who are growing the fruit of righteousness are those who are honestly praying, "Others, Lord, yes others, let this my motto be. May I live for others that I may live like thee."

Set Goals That Will Bring Glory To God
When Realized

The third principle for goal setting is that Christians should set only goals with potential for glorifying God.

Paul's words in verse 31 remind us of our highest mission. "So whether you eat or drink or whatever you do, do it all for the glory of God."

It is appropriate to ask of ourselves before entering into any endeavor, "Can I do this to honor God?" There are three questions to consider when attempting to determine the answer to that question.

(1) Is the action I am considering consistent with the commands and principles of God's Word?

We acknowledge God's greatness when we obey Him. Our obedience is our testimony that we believe God to be who He says He is and capable of everything the Bible says He is capable.

(2) Does the action I am considering cast God in a positive light?

A friend of mine who was an Indiana State Policeman told me that he was reminded regularly by his superiors, "When you wear that uniform, you represent the State Police. It's your responsibility to behave in a fashion that will enhance the reputation of state law enforcement." As a representative of the State Police he was responsible for maintaining the credibility of that agency by his personal integrity.

Second Corinthians 5:20-21 presents a huge challenge to Christians: "We are therefore Christ's ambassadors, as though God were making his appeal through us....God made him who had no sin to be sin for us, so that in him we might become the righteousness of God."

As ambassadors we represent the Lord, and as His representatives we are responsible to behave in a way that affirms the credibility of the One we represent.

(3) Does the action I am considering promote God's cause?

As servants and children of the Lord, we are obligated to evaluate our goals in light of the potential of those goals to help build up God's people on this earth. God is glorified as His purpose is exalted. We are His agents, comissioned to carry out His purposes not our own, and that should be our major consideration as we set goals that bring glory to God.

Perhaps the exhortation of the psalmist should be kept before us as we consider the goals that will guide our lives. He wrote, "Ascribe to the Lord, O mighty ones, ascribe to the Lord glory and strength. Ascribe to the Lord the glory due his name..." (Psalm 29:1-2).

Set Goals That Are In Keeping With Christ's Example

The fourth principle for goal setting is to set goals that are consistent with the example of Christ. In I Corinthians 11:1, Paul exhorts, "Follow my example, as I follow the example of Christ."

Charles Sheldon's classic Christian novel, *In His Steps*, is about a group of people who dared to ask the question, "What would Jesus do?" That is the question that the person striving for fruitfulness will ask often. Most of the hard decisions of life can be made by simply following Jesus' example. We can trust His example, for He made no mistakes. Paul reminds us of that in II Corinthians 5:21, "God made him who had no sin...."

To say as Paul did, that it is safe to follow us because our actions are an example of what Jesus would do, is a bold statement. A worthy ambition for you and me is to so live that that statement can truthfully be made...and so that others see the truth of it.

Set Visionary Goals

A fifth principle for goal setting is to set goals that are consistent with our faith. We serve a powerful God. Appropriate goals reflect that power.

In one TV commercial aired regularly a few years back,

a young woman, who has obviously been running in the rain, comes into the kitchen where her husband has some hot soup waiting for her. Her comments make it obvious she is worried about the upcoming marathon. The husband lovingly says, "I'm surprised you are worried about finishing."

"Finishing?" she says with a smile, "I'm worried about *winning.*"

Her attitude is commendable. We accomplish the most when we set our goals high. How often are we so confident of finishing the race that we fail to be concerned about winning the race of life for Christ?

Theodore Roosevelt said, "Far better it is to dare mighty things, to win glorious triumphs, even though checkered by failure, than to take rank with those poor spirits who neither enjoy much nor suffer much, because they live in the gray twilight that knows not victory nor defeat."

How does one attain visionary faith? There is an account in the book of Nehemiah that should give us a hint. Nehemiah asked a passing traveler about conditions back in Jerusalem. What he heard was not good news. The people remaining in Jerusalem after the exile were in trouble. The walls were down and the gates had been burned. Discouragement was rampant.

Nehemiah records, "When I heard these things, I sat down and wept. For some days I mourned and fasted and prayed before the God of heaven" (Nehemiah 1:4).

Later, we find Nehemiah in Jerusalem. He reports, "I had not told anyone what my God had put in my heart to do for Jerusalem" (2:12). What did God put in Nehemiah's heart? God gave Nehemiah a burden to rebuild the walls of the city, but it is important for us to note that Nehemiah had such a goal only after he heard the need. Then he had faith in God and a compassion for his people which motivated him to fast and pray.

A close relationship with God develops only as we spend time with God. A strong devotional life is essential to spiritual vision, for it is there that we come to know God's heart.

I was eight or nine years old when I got my first air rifle. It took only a little practice and I was hitting targets from a close range, but distant marks were another matter. My older cousin, attempting to help me hit the distant targets, explained that the air pressure produced by the rifle could carry the BB on a straight line for only a limited distance. If I hoped to hit the distant targets, I needed to aim higher. I raised my air rifle and carefully took aim a foot above the target. I missed the target again and my cousin advised, "Aim higher." I was still a little short and again he instructed, "Aim a little higher." This time I jumped for joy as I hit my target almost dead center.

I have discovered my cousin's advice to be good advice for every area of my life. Quality spiritual fruit is attained by aiming high.

PRINCIPLES TO PONDER:
1. Goals which reflect a Christ-like purpose will produce the right kind of fruit.

2. Specific goals are most beneficial.

3. I Corinthians 10:23–11:1 reveal some valuable considerations for setting goals.

4. Some goals are destructive.

5. The best goals are goals that reflect our faith.

6. Our devotional life will determine our spiritual goals.

PRACTICING THE PRINCIPLES:
1. Put on paper your three most prominent goals, then evaluate them in light of I Corinthians 10:23–11:1.

2. Decide in what direction you would want your life to go if there were absolutely no obstacles or circumstances preventing it. Talk with God about that dream every day for at least two weeks.

3. Read the book of Jonah, listing the factors that seemed to hinder Jonah, and then the factors that helped him determine the direction of his life and ministry.

chapter three

Choose the Right Attitude

Two soldiers of fortune were offered $200 for every enemy soldier they captured. They searched for several days with no success. They could not find even a trace of an enemy soldier. The two discouraged men went to sleep by their campfire one night almost ready to give up. That night one of the men was awakened when he felt cold steel against his throat. He looked up to see the biggest enemy soldier he had ever seen straddled over him holding a huge machete across his throat. However, that was not the worst of it. Enemy soldiers were all around him. They completely surrounded the camp. There must have been at least a thousand of them.

As he lay there with enemy soldiers all around him, the blade of the machete almost puncturing the flesh of his throat, he very carefully punched his partner beside him and whispered, "Josh, Josh, wake up. We're rich."

That man had mastered the art of seeing life's circumstances in a positive light. He could see the bright side even in the most desperate of situations.

Fruit that glorifies God is produced by those who approach life from this kind of positive perspective. The Christian, of all people, can be confident and positive. Most of us, though, have some trouble doing that. We can develop such an attitude by learning three important lessons.

Look Beyond Self

No Christian is doomed to spiritual mediocrity. Something extraordinary is always within reach. There is nothing beyond the capability of one in the Lord's will. "I can do everything through him who gives me strength" (Philippians 4:13).

The first key to a godly attitude is learning to go beyond self. The beauty of being a Christian is that we do not have to depend on self. Paul talked about that in his letter to the Philippians. He wrote, "Whatever you have learned or received or heard from me, or seen in me—put it into practice" (4:9).

Paul obviously did not suffer from lack of confidence. Where did he get that confidence? He had received the best education available in his day from Gamaliel (Acts 22:3). The book of Acts leaves little doubt that Paul was a man of extraordinary ability.

But was his education, background, or ability responsible for his remarkable feats? Not at all! Paul admitted it was *through Christ* that he could do all things. Paul made himself available to the Lord and the Lord took it from there.

Christ living in him made it possible for him to move

ahead in whatever direction the Lord chose for him. Paul lived and acted in the belief that God was in control. By making himself available to God, he accepted power beyond himself for the tasks ahead. Paul did not accept "I can't" as a valid response. He probably refused to ask himself the question, "Can I?" Rather, I hear him asking, *Does the Lord want it?* He knew that where there is conformity to the will of the Lord, there is always power beyond self for whatever lies ahead.

One preacher admitted, "I struggled in my ministry until I realized *I* could not do it—but God could. Victories started coming when I learned to depend on Him rather than on my own abilities."

An amazing lady once told me, "The Lord has done things through me I would never have dreamed I could do before becoming a Christian." It is still true that the Lord is more interested in our availability rather than just our ability. It seems that He chose His apostles on the basis of their willingness rather than by their talents. He still chooses disciples by that method.

Acts 4:13 tells us about the Sanhedrin's impression of two of the apostles. "When they saw the courage of Peter and John and realized that they were unschooled, ordinary men, they were astonished and they took note that these men had been with Jesus."

By the standards of the Sanhedrin, Peter and John were uneducated, with only ordinary ability, but in spite of that, they so affected the people of Jerusalem that the religious leaders were astonished.

How could it happen? The answer is, "They had been with Jesus!" Jesus told them, "But you will receive power when the Holy Spirit comes on you; and you will be my witnesses in Jerusalem, and in all Judea and Samaria, and to the ends of the earth" (Acts 1:8).

Peter, John, and the other apostles had a power beyond themselves for doing the Lord's work. We have the same Holy Spirit living within us. With the promise of such power, there is no reason to shy away from even the most difficult task. We have the same potential to reach our world for Christ as Peter, John, and Paul.

A man who has taught many aspiring young preachers, once said, "Brilliance and exceptional ability sometimes get in the way of our spiritual achievement." He explained, "We must look to the Lord rather than depending on our own ability. Great ability and learning will take us only a short distance at best, but the Lord can take us all the way."

Ability is a blessing. Education is important. However, high achievers are not always blessed with great ability or an extensive education. I have grown to believe the truth of a statement I heard a Bible teacher make many years ago, "Whatever you have plus the Lord's power is enough to do the job one hundred percent of the time."

Trust God's Power

A second key to a godly attitude is learning to trust God's power. God's power is available to those who trust Him enough to use it. Isaiah wrote, "...in quietness and trust is your strength" (30:15).

I worked on the college maintenance crew while I was a student. One day I had the experience of using the "harness" designed for power company employees who climbed poles for a living. I climbed up a pole to put a security light in place. I got to the spot where the light was to be fixed. But I could not, for the life of me, bring myself to trust the belt enough to lean back and allow it to support me while I worked. My supervisor impatiently cried out from below, "Use the belt."

I had tested the belt before climbing up the pole. I knew it would hold my weight. I had looked at it carefully to make sure it was not defective, but for some reason I refused to trust it. My experience on that pole is similar to the experience of some people who know full well the Lord is sufficient, but still find it difficult to trust Him with the big and small things of life.

I can think of several reasons why some people might find it difficult to put trust in God's power.

(1) We will not trust anyone whom we do not know. When we have not observed God's power close up, on a personal, daily basis, we will not trust it.

(2) We will not trust God's power when we focus on the failure around us and believe that weakness is the rule. We forget that we cannot base our beliefs about God on what we observe in people.

(3) We tend to distrust God's power when we evaluate it in light of our own ability. We are reluctant to respond to God's power when we attribute our weakness to God's lack of power.

(4) We may not be able to trust God's power because we have been conditioned to believe that to trust someone else is an indication of weakness. That seems to be a prevalent philosophy in our society today.

(5) We may not trust God's power simply because we have not been taught to do so.

Our God is an all-powerful God. He caused the waters of the Red Sea to roll back, allowing the children of Israel to cross on dry ground. He caused the walls of Jericho to fall at the sound of a trumpet, producing a victory for

His people. He created the heavens and earth in six days. Our Lord often demonstrated His power during his thirty-three years on earth. He calmed the sea, walked on water, and cleansed lepers. He raised Lazarus from the dead and healed the woman who touched His garment. The grave could not hold Him.

What power! The exciting news is that the Lord is just as powerful today. And we can be just as close to Him as any of the people or events we read about in the Bible.

Jesus said to His disciples, "With God all things are possible" (Matthew 19:26).

The psalmist wrote, "Those who trust in the Lord are like Mount Zion, which cannot be shaken but endures forever" (Psalm 125:1).

Trust God's Love

The third key for a godly attitude is learning to trust God's love. Matthew's Gospel tells us that a man with leprosy came and knelt before Jesus saying, "Lord, if you are willing, you can make me clean" (8:2).

That man knew Jesus had the power to heal him of his disease. Perhaps he had heard or seen what Jesus did on behalf of other people with similar needs. Matthew does not tell us why that leper had faith in Jesus' ability to heal, but there is no doubt he believed in the power of Jesus.

The agony of being afflicted with leprosy in the time of Jesus went beyond physical suffering. Those who had leprosy were considered unclean. So as not to infect others, they were forced to live as outcasts. They often lived in caves outside the villages. They were not permitted contact with *normal people.*

This particular leper acknowledged the power of the Lord

to heal him, but, at the same time, having experienced re-
jection from his neighbors, he seemed to wonder if the
Lord cared enough about him to use that power. Jesus quickly
dispeled any doubts about His caring nature by reaching
out and touching the afflicted man. He said, "I am willing....Be
clean!" The man was cured immediately (v. 3).

That leper's heart must have sung when Jesus dared to
touch him. A *clean man*, a Teacher with crowds following
after him, had actually cared enough to touch him. What
a blessing that must have been to one who was often reminded
of his condition by cries of "unclean" as people ran away
from him. This Jesus recognized his physical problem but
reacted to it differently than others. He reached out to him
and He cured him. Could there be any doubt about the
love of the Lord?

A woman I'll call Beth endured a rough childhood. Her
stepfather sexually abused her. Later, a neighbor for whom
she babysat took advantage of her in the same way. When
she first came to see me she considered herself "unclean."
Her marriage was in shambles. She had no confidence. Beth
was a Christian, but she said to me, "I don't feel at all
spiritual." She explained, "I want to find the joy that others
have found in Christ, but it seems to be impossible for me."

Beth did not doubt the ability of the Lord to "straighten
out" her life, and she wanted to serve the Lord. Her problem
was that she had been abused all her life. She had difficulty
believing anyone, including the Lord, cared enough about
her to actually want to help.

How can we doubt the love of the Father when we believe
John 3:16? "For God so loved the world that he gave his
one and only Son, that whoever believes in him shall not
perish but have eternal life."

How can we doubt the love of Jesus the Son when we

read in Scripture, "Greater love has no one than this, that one lay down his life for his friends" (John 15:13).

One who regularly reads the Bible, believing it to be truth, cannot doubt for long the magnitude of God's power nor the depth of His love. His power and love are everywhere between Genesis and Revelation.

A godly attitude is easy to achieve when we trust both God's power and His caring nature. God is *able* and *willing*. All kinds of new possibilities open up to us when we honestly grasp the truth of that statement.

Jump With Faith

The events of a particular day in my childhood have remained with me for many years. I was eleven years old. The two boys with me were several years my senior. We came to a stream. The two older boys easily jumped it. Then they coaxed me from the other side, "You can do it. Come on."

I backed up and ran toward the creek, all the while wondering, *Can I do it?* As I approached the creek there was no doubt left in my mind. I knew I *couldn't* do it! In the split second I had left, I could not decide whether to jump or stop. You guessed it! I landed right in the middle of the stream. I jumped and at the same time tried to stop. There I stood, knee deep in water and mud—the fruit of uncertainty! But the story does not end there. A few days later I jumped that same creek, this time with confidence and determination, and I had no problem clearing it.

When we approach life with the certainty that we have Someone greater than ourselves—when we approach it with trust in God's power and love—we will try and accomplish feats that others might consider impossible. A positive, godly attitude toward life will help keep us out of the muck and mire of life while enabling us to be of maximum usefulness to the Lord.

PRINCIPLES TO PONDER:

1. God the Holy Spirit dwells within the Christian, giving him/her a power beyond self.

2. Fruitfulness is enhanced more by availability than ability.

3. God's power is obvious to us when we trust enough to depend upon it.

4. Nothing is beyond God's ability.

5. It is important to believe in the power of God, but equally important to believe He cares enough to use that power on our behalf.

6. Fruitfulness is accelerated or slowed by the quality of our faith in who God is.

PRACTICING THE PRINCIPLES:

1. Talk with someone whose faith has triggered accomplishments seemingly beyond his or her ability; ask about the development of that faith.

2. Sit down with paper and pen and list every proof of God's love that comes to your mind. Read that list every day for two weeks and add to it as new proofs pop into your mind.

3. Read Genesis 12–20, listing the actions of Abraham prompted by his trust in God's power and caring nature. Then, evaluate the past five years of your life, listing those actions that were possible only because you trusted in God's power and His love.

chapter four

Choose the Right Blueprint

Paul wrote to Timothy about the benefits Scripture offers those striving to live a life that glorifies God. He said, "All Scripture is God-breathed and is useful for teaching, rebuking, correcting and training in righteousness, so that the man of God may be thoroughly equipped for every good work" (II Timothy 3:16-17).

What The Bible Has To Offer

Those verses reveal that Scripture provides three ingredients extremely important for the fruit-bearing Christian.

The Bible provides motivation for fruitfulness. Paul wrote that Scripture is "God-breathed." Men penned the words, but God's Holy Spirit directed their thoughts and words.

Each one is from the mouth and heart of God. An older preacher once suggested to me, "Danny, if you want people to sit up and take note when you quote Scripture, don't tell them Paul said or Peter said, tell them, *God said.*"

The expectations of others did not always motivate me as a boy. For instance, I didn't pay much attention to my sister when she told me to be home by 5:00. Her expectations didn't impress me much. After all, she was two years younger than I. What right did she have to tell me what to do? However, when my father told me to be home by 5:00, I was there by 4:45. He *did* have the right to tell me what to do. His instructions carried some weight. His expectations motivated me.

The Bible teaches that Christians are to produce. Since the Bible is "God-breathed," it is *God* who instructs His children to produce. Those expectations should carry some weight since they come from the supreme authority of our heavenly Father.

The Bible provides still other kinds of motivation. When we get serious about studying God's Word, we find that God's love is the golden strand running from Genesis to Revelation. We stand amazed at His grandeur which Scripture so eloquently reveals. How can we not be motivated by exposure to such realizations?

The Bible directs our quest for fruitfulness. God's Word gives us two sets of directions.

(1) It directs us *away* from that which will hinder us. Paul stated that Scripture is useful for *rebuking*. It makes us aware of the sin in our lives. God instructs us to abstain from certain actions, not because He wants to establish who is boss, but because He wants the best for us. God's Word points us away from that which would void our efforts.

(2) The Bible directs us *toward* that which will help

to increase our fruitfulness. Paul wrote that Scripture is useful for "training in righteousness." The Bible is not simply a book of "thou shalt nots." It gives instructions on how God wants us to live, and it serves as a guideline for achieving that kind of existence.

The psalmist spoke of this value of Scripture when he wrote, "Your word is a lamp to my feet and a light for my path" (119:105).

The Bible equips us for fruitfulness. Paul stated that Scripture was given "So the man of God may be thoroughly equipped for every good work."

What equipment do we need to be fruitful? Certainly most of us recognize the critical importance of faith. How then can we be equipped with faith? The answer is found in Romans 10:17. "Faith comes from hearing the message, and the message is heard through the word of Christ." Faith starts with exposure to God's Word.

But the equipping value of the Bible goes beyond even that. The Word of God is the sword of the Spirit (Ephesians 6:17). The Holy Spirit works through the Word of God as a weapon against Satan who stands as the killer frost to the Christian's fruitfulness. When we put on the "armor of God," the Bible equips us by becoming the only offensive weapon available to us.

The Bible also equips us with needed encouragement, confidence, instructions, and much more. It is the Christian's equipping manual.

How To Benefit From The Bible

The Bible, handled responsibly, will produce quality fruit. Those who get the most from God's Word—*read the Word.*

The boss gave me a manual on the very first night I

worked at a new job. He explained, "Read this manual and you will never have any doubt about what we expect of you. Your success on this job will, to a large extent, depend on how much attention you give this manual." Taking his remarks seriously, I studied that manual thoroughly. I determined to please my new supervisor from the very first moment on the job.

Paul suggested to Timothy that he needed to spend some time in the Manual to please his "Boss." He wrote, "Study to shew thyself approved unto God, a workman that needeth not to be ashamed, rightly dividing the word of truth" (II Timothy 2:15, KJV).

We are to allow the Bible to speak to us. One lady, faithful in her church attendance, often greeted the preacher at the door after the service with such comments as, "You really gave *them* what they needed to hear today," or "That ought to make *them* think." It was always *them* and never *us*.

The preacher told me that more than once he was tempted to respond to such comments by saying, "Why, Alice (not her real name), I prepared that message just for you." Evidently, she was never struck with the possibility that the preacher's messages from God's Word were for her as well as others. How often are we guilty of that?

It is good to search the Scriptures to find passages that will help a friend through a crisis. I'm glad friends have done that for me. However, we must not neglect to read the Word of God to hear what He has for *us*.

I once complimented a friend on the beautiful job he did on a piece of woodwork. He humbly accepted the compliment saying, "I listened to my father." He explained, "My dad was a master wood craftsman, and I learned all I know about woodwork from him."

Our heavenly Father is the "expert in life." When we listen to His instructions and put them to work, we will build beautiful lives that cannot help but be fruitful.

Then, the Bible is to be read for understanding. The Bible has no purpose if it is impossible to understand; however, more than one person has said to me, "I read the Bible, but I don't understand it."

John tells us we can understand the Bible, "As for you, the anointing you received from him remains in you, and you do not need anyone to teach you. But as His anointing teaches you about all things and as that anointing is real, not counterfeit—just as it has taught you, remain in him" (I John 2:27).

What is John's point? The Lord has equipped us with the Holy Spirit and with the Bible. God's Holy Spirit gives us the help we need to understand God's Word. When we always start our Bible reading sessions with prayer, we can petition God's help to understand what we are about to read.

Plus, the Bible is to be read often.

"I don't have time to seriously read the Bible," is a frequent complaint I hear. Most of us can identify with that since our time must be chopped up for so many seemingly important activities. We'll deal with the problem of time in another chapter. The one fact we must remember here is that regular Bible study is as important to our spiritual health as eating regular, balanced meals is to our physical health.

Remember the Word. The psalmist set a good example for us. He wrote, "I have hidden your word in my heart that I might not sin against you" (119:11).

We best put God's Word to work in our lives when we can live and breathe it as part of our memory banks. We cannot always take out a Bible to see how God would have us deal with a particular situation. We can react correctly in difficult situations only if the Word is already implanted in our hearts and minds.

Scripture memorization is one of the most beneficial endeavors we will ever undertake. I have learned that a three by five card can be a most useful tool for learning Scripture. Write a passage on a card. The card can be put in a pocket or purse and taken out for study during previously wasted moments. When that passage has been learned, the card can be replaced with another. It is surprising how much of God's Word can be committed to memory through this method.

Review the Word. Joshua instructed the children of Israel, "Do not let this Book of the Law depart from your mouth; meditate on it day and night, so that you may be careful to do everything written in it. That you will be prosperous and successful" (Joshua 1:8).

Joshua's use of the word "meditate" reminds us that we are to dwell on God's Word. The Word should be pondered and digested. To read the Word and then forget it will not contribute much to our growth or to our fruit-bearing. Growth can best be accomplished when we read the Word, memorize it, and meditate upon it.

Obey the Word. A man testified, "I ran from Bible conference to Bible conference. I attended three Bible studies every week. I thought I could make points with God by learning His Word. I was convinced God would overlook the sin in my life because of the knowledge in my head."

But it isn't possible.

The children of Israel at Jericho learned the advantage of obeying God's instructions. They crossed the Jordan into the Promised Land, but they faced an immediate, gigantic problem. They had to conquer Jericho before they could move on, but it was fortified with a strong wall.

In Joshua 6:2-6 we read God's instructions to Joshua.

> Then the Lord said to Joshua, "See, I have delivered
> Jericho into your hands, along with its king and
> its fighting men. March around the city once with
> all the armed men. Do this for six days. Have
> seven priests carry trumpets of rams' horns in
> front of the ark. On the seventh day, march around
> the city seven times, with the priests blowing the
> trumpets. When you hear them sound a long blast
> on the trumpets, have all the people give a loud
> shout; then the wall of the city will collapse and
> the people will go up, every man straight in."

The instructions were strange. But Joshua led the people
to follow God's instructions. On the seventh day, when
the trumpets sounded and the people shouted, the walls
collapsed and every man charged in. The city was taken.
They won an extraordinary victory (6:20) because they
obeyed God—even when His directions made no human
sense. They also learned that God gives victory to those
who obey Him.

Christians who know and obey God's will are sure to
reap a bountiful harvest that will glorify God. James warned
us about dependence upon knowledge alone. He wrote,
"Anyone who listens to the word, but does not
do what it says is like a man who looks at his
face in a mirror and, after looking at himself, goes away
and immediately forgets what he looks like. But the man
who looks intently into the perfect law that gives freedom,
and continues to do this, not forgetting what he has heard,
but doing it—he will be blessed in what he does" (James
1:23-26).

We do not gain anything by looking into a mirror and

refusing to make the adjustments the mirror demands. We do not help ourselves when we study a road map if we refuse to travel in the direction which it shows to be the right way. We do not grow spiritually unless we read the Bible and then obey its directions.

There are many illustrations of this truth in the Bible. Noah and his family were saved from the flood when Noah obeyed God's instruction in building the ark (Genesis 6). Naaman was healed of leprosy after following the instructions of God's prophet (II Kings 5:1-14). A blind man was healed when he dipped himself in the pool of Siloam as Jesus instructed (John 9:1-7). The Bible is full of such examples. None of them logical by human understanding. All of them miraculous examples of God's power revealed in the simple things.

Notice that God gave Joshua *specific* instructions on how to conquer Jericho. He told him how many times to march around the city. He told him how many days He wanted them to march. He gave him the order in which He wanted them to march. He told him who He wanted to carry the trumpets and the ark of the covenant.

Likewise, God gave Noah specific instructions for building the ark. He told him, "Build it out of gopher wood" and gave him the exact dimensions. God also gave him specific instructions concerning who and what He wanted to board the ark (Genesis 6 and 7).

The servant of God's prophet told Naaman to dip himself in a particular body of water—the Jordan. The servant told him, "Dip yourself seven times" (not just four or five, but seven). God healed him when he obeyed the prophet's specific instructions (II Kings 5:1-14).

With a twinkle in his eyes, my grandfather said to me while trying to teach me to drive, "When you come to a curve in the road, you have to turn the steering wheel, and it does make a difference which way you turn it."

Specifics are important in driving, and they are important in serving. The fruit of righteousness only grows when we hear and respond to God's specifics. When we come to the curves in life, it does make a difference which way we turn.

I once mixed some Kool-Aid mistakenly using salt instead of sugar. It took only one swallow to convince me that specifics do make a difference. Our endeavors can be bitter, sour, or just out of kilter when we ignore God's specifics. On the other hand, fruitfulness will be the result when we do exactly as God instructs in His Word.

PRINCIPLES TO PONDER:

1. *All* Scripture is inspired by God.

2. The Bible motivates, directs, and equips us for the highest endeavors of life.

3. The Holy Spirit helps us understand the Bible.

4. Scripture is most helpful to us when we "hide it in our hearts."

5. Bible knowledge is most useful when we put it to work in our lives.

6. The *specifics* of God's Word cannot be ignored.

PRACTICING THE PRINCIPLES:

1. If you have not already done so, enter into an organized personal study of a particular book of the Bible.

2. There are several plans to be found in most Christian bookstores for reading the Bible through in a year. Obtain one and start a year-long journey through God's Word.

3. Read Nehemiah 8, then write a paragraph based on that chapter about the power of God's Word.

____

chapter five

____

Choose to Exert the Right Effort

"He is not short on dreams," a concerned mother remarked about her son. "It's effort he seems to have trouble with."

Dreams are certainly an advantage to those who want to serve and glorify God, but more than dreams is required. It requires the right kind of effort to produce the right kind of spiritual results. These five approaches to our work will help trigger maximum fruit production.

Work Hard

Hard work produces godly results.

I was a twelve-year-old Boy Scout excited about adding a hiking merit badge to my collection of colorful badges. I checked out the requirements and responded with a degree

49

of surprise when I discovered, among other things, that I had to take two five-mile hikes and one twenty-mile hike in order to earn it. I carefully evaluated those requirements, considering all the walking I would have to do. I thought about the blisters I was sure to have on my feet and decided the hiking merit badge wasn't for me. I rationalized, "Anyone can get a hiking merit badge, all you have to do is walk." The truth, of course, was that I did not pursue that badge because of my adolescent lazy streak. I could not get excited about doing all that walking.

Laziness is an obstacle to any achievement. Plato said, "If a man would move the world, he must first move himself." Thomas Edison told a friend, "Genius is one percent inspiration and ninety-nine percent perspiration."

What enables people like Edison to reach such amazing levels of discovery and productivity? It may not be as much their brilliance as their attitude. They are not afraid of hard work or of the possiblity of failure. They expend tremendous energy and get big results.

Hard work is an extension of faith. Reading the eleventh chapter of Hebrews is like walking through God's hall of achievers. A walk through that "faith chapter" brings us face to face with some of God's greatest servants. The writer commends each person mentioned there for an active faith— faith that motivated them to do something for the Lord...no matter how hard or how great the sacrifice.

"By faith Abel *offered...*" (v. 4). "By faith Noah...*built* an ark..." (v. 7). "By faith Abraham...*obeyed and went*" (v. 8). The list includes a number of others motivated to action by genuine faith.

Our works are also an extension of our love. God demonstrated that principle. "For God so loved the world that he gave his one and only Son..." (John 3:16). God was motivated by love to do something about our lost state.

Genuine love is like that. We have a desire to "do" for those we love. James 2:8 adds, "If you really keep the royal law found in Scripture, 'Love your neighbor as yourself.'" Later in that chapter, he adds, "What good is it, my brothers, if a man claims to have faith but has no deeds?...Show me your faith without deeds, and I will show you my faith by what I do" (2:14,18).

If hard work results from faith and love, then the greater our faith and love, the more likely we are to have a willing spirit toward work that serves our Lord. The other side is that our works are a pretty good gauge of the magnitude of our faith and the depth of our love.

Work Joyously

Work approached with a joyous spirit will get the best results. Paul, in his epistle to the Philippians, speaks to us about being glad in the Lord's work:

> Do everything without complaining or arguing,
> so that you may become blameless and pure,
> children of God without fault in a crooked and
> depraved generation, in which you shine like stars
> in the universe as you hold out the word of life—
> in order that I may boast on the day of Christ
> that I did not run or labor for nothing. But even
> if I am being poured out like a drink offering on
> the sacrifice and service coming from your faith,
> I am glad and rejoice with all of you. So you
> too should be glad and rejoice with me.
>
> (2:14-18)

Paul literally poured all of himself into his labors, and

he did so with gladness and joy. He did not complain about having to work hard. He suggested to the Philippians—and to us—that his example was only what God expected.

The writer of Hebrews very effectively reminds us of an even better example. Hebrews 12:2 says, "Let us fix our eyes on Jesus, the author and perfecter of our faith, who for the joy set before him endured the cross, scorning its shame, and sat down at the right hand of the throne of God."

There are three motivating factors for gladly serving the Lord. (1) We can find joy in the Lord's work *because of whom we are serving*. It is a privilege to serve the One who gave His life for us, the King of Kings and Lord of Lords.

(2) We can find joy in the Lord's work *because of its purpose*. Jesus said, "For the Son of Man came to seek and to save what was lost" (Luke 19:10). That is the ultimate purpose of all the work we do for the Lord. First Corinthians 10:31 adds another element to our purpose, "So…whatever you do, do it all for the glory of God."

(3) Still another factor contributing to joy in the Lord's work is *the reward*. The Lord could have sent angels to do His work on earth. He could simply accept our service as His due. But instead He promises, "Do not throw away your confidence; it will be richly rewarded" (Hebrews 10:35). "This is what the Lord says: '…your work will be rewarded'" (Jeremiah 31:16).

Work Lovingly
Work approached with a spirit of loving excellence produces the best results.

In a high school wood shop class, I watched a fellow

student put a lot of extra effort into the bookcase on which he was working. He worked for several weeks until the finish was perfect. One day I asked him, "Dwight, why are you so particular with that bookcase?"

I'll never forget his answer. He proudly announced, "Because it's for Mom and Dad."

He did the best job he could because it was a gift of love for the two people in the world who loved him most. How could he give them less than his best?

God loves us most. He is our Creator. Through the gift of His Son, God is responsible for our salvation. The Lord blesses us abundantly. Doesn't such love demand our very best?

God instructed David to build an altar on the threshing floor of Araunah the Jebusite. Araunah saw the king and his escort coming, so he went out and bowed down before David.

Araunah asked, "Why has my lord the king come to his servant?"

David answered, "To buy your threshing floor so I can build an altar to the Lord, that the plague on the people may be stopped."

Araunah then said to David, "Let my lord the king take whatever pleases him and offer it up. Here are oxen for the burnt offering, and here are threshing sledges and ox yokes for the wood. O king, Araunah gives all this to the king."

David responded to Araunah's generous offer by stating a very important principle: "No, I insist on paying you for it. I will not sacrifice to the Lord my God burnt offerings that cost me nothing" (II Samuel 24:18-25).

How we approach our responsibilities to God reveal a lot about how we view Him. If we see Him as the loving

Creator and sovereign God of the universe, the almighty King of our lives, we will refuse to offer shoddy effort on His behalf. We will lovingly sacrifice in order to give Him our best effort.

Work Persistently

Work characterized by persistence leads to godly results.

Those who approach the Lord's work with relentless persistence, even when the work is not easy, find the richest lives.

When I was in high school, I decided I wanted to be on the track team. I was not a gifted runner. In fact, I ran the hundred-yard dash in the relatively slow time of about twelve seconds. I had to put out of my mind any thought of running the sprints. I would have to be an endurance runner in order to compete. I chose the two-mile run. Since it was the longest run, speed was least essential to competing than in any other track event.

Searching for help, I read the advice of a successful endurance runner: "When it starts to hurt, run a little faster," he suggested.

Now that's good advice, I thought. *It always hurts when I run the two mile and the faster I run, the quicker I finish. The quicker I finish, the quicker it stops hurting.*

I often won the two mile event because I accelerated a little each time I felt pain.

I have tried to carry that principle with me through my life. When it hurts, run a little faster. When the going gets rough, try harder. When the job is difficult, instead of quitting, work with more diligence.

Once when I complained about the difficulty of doing the Lord's work, a friend reminded me, "A smooth sea never made a good sailor." He was right. A sailor who does not experience some rough water will never develop his skills to their fullest potential. If our work for the Lord is always easy, we will never sharpen our faith, our spiritual skills, or our commitment.

The advantage of a difficult task is that it will likely force us to seek the Lord's help. A grand old saint told me, "The best thing the Lord did for me was give me a difficult ministry in my early years. I learned the most and I grew the fastest in those days," he said.

Work Smart

Work approached with common sense produces godly results.

Common sense dictates that we get involved in those aspects of the Lord's work for which we have an aptitude— a God-given ability.

Apparently, members of the church at Corinth boastfully exhibited their spiritual gifts. From the information we have in Paul's first epistle to them, we might assume they were comparing gifts and claiming, "You are inferior because you cannot do what I do."

Paul condemned that kind of attitude. When he compared the body of Christ to the physical body, he wrote:

> Now the body is not made up of one part but of many. If the foot should say, "Because I am not a hand, I do not belong to the body," it would not for that reason cease to be part of the body. And if the ear should say, "Because I am not an eye, I do not belong to the body," it would not for that reason cease to be part of the body. If the whole body were an eye, where would the

sense of hearing be? If the whole body were an ear, where would the sense of smell be? But in fact God has arranged the parts in the body, every one of them, just as he wanted them to be. If they were all one part, where would the body be? As it is, there are many parts, but one body.

(I Corinthians 12:14-20)

The Lord gave Christians different gifts in order that His composite body would function properly. The church would be in trouble if everyone were gifted identically. One way to determine the areas in which the Lord wants us to serve is to determine what gifts He gave us.

Normally, we do not take a lot of time to decide which functions our hands or feet will perform, we just naturally use them to do that for which they are designed.

Shouldn't we just naturally do for the Lord that for which we are built? Such an approach would enable us to avoid a lot of frustration and discouragement, the kind that comes when we choose to serve in areas where we are not gifted.

That sounds simple, but we need to approach this philosophy with caution. It provides a good way out when we are looking for one. When we don't want to pay the price involved in a particular task, we may be tempted to reason, "I don't have that gift." It can become an excuse.

We also need to be on guard against allowing this philosophy to desensitize us to the Lord's will when He is leading us in a different direction than the one we want to go or where our apparent abilities lie. The Lord called Moses to lead the children of Israel out of bondage even though Moses felt strongly that he did not have the right abilities for the job (Exodus 4).

We can also use common sense to balance our work because the Lord's work has many facets.

For example, parents are doing the Lord's work when they "train up their children in the way they should go" (Proverbs 22:6). Lifestyle evangelism is also the Lord's work (Philippians 1:21, Romans 12). Working hard for the Lord can include caring for widows and orphans (James 1:27) or fighting discrimination (James 2:1-4). It's balance that grows the best fruit possible. We'll consider it in greater detail in another chapter.

My Grandpa Jordan was the hardest working man I ever knew. One day as we cleaned out a chicken house, he said something I've never forgotten: "Danny, a person who is not willing to work cannot expect much of life."

He was right.

When we work wholeheartedly for the Lord, approaching His work with the right attitude, we can expect our God, who is "able to make all grace abound to you…will enlarge the harvest of your righteousness" (II Corinthians 9:8-10).

PRINCIPLES TO PONDER:

1. Hard work is an extension of our faith and love for Christ.

2. Joy fills our work for the Lord when we are keenly aware of whom we are serving.

3. The Lord deserves our very best efforts.

4. The best response to a difficult task is to give more effort.

5. We are most effective in the Lord's work when we discover our gifts, allowing them to determine the nature of our work.

6. There are many avenues and places of service in the Lord's work.

PRACTICING THE PRINCIPLES:

1. Choose a special project which you feel will honor the Lord and invest at least two hours a week for the next month in that project.

2. Study James 2:14-25 using at least two commentaries and three Bible translations. Write a brief summary of what you believe God is telling you in that passage of Scripture.

3. Ask your minister and other godly people you respect to help you identify your "spiritual gift(s)." When you are confident it has been identified, ask the Lord to open a door that will let you use it for His glory.

chapter six

Choose the Right Companionship

I have known no couple more vibrantly alive in service for the Lord than Todd and Jenny. They were relatively new Christians when I met them, but already they were obviously people who were diligently striving to make those choices that would enable them to be strong witnesses of the transforming power of the Lord.

I was fascinated by how far they had come in a short period of time and told them so.

Jenny responded to my praise by giving much of the credit to another couple who had developed close ties with them and maintained those ties throughout their Christian lives.

"Steve and Dee deserve much of the credit," she offered. "They stuck with us through thick and thin. They loved us when we were not very lovable. They helped us overcome our doubts. They taught us, and they were there for us in the difficult times."

Jenny has since gone to be with the Lord. My wife and I traveled two hundred and fifty miles to attend her funeral and to spend a couple of hours ministering to Todd. As it turned out, he ministered to us.

There was standing room only at the funeral, and we were told that hundreds of people had stood in the rain for hours the previous night to pay their respects. Almost every person to whom we spoke that day mentioned times when Jenny was a blessing to them. Her short life had, indeed, been fruitful.

Hundreds of people were recipients of Jenny's ministry, and, by her own account, it was a credit to the fellowship she and Todd had enjoyed with Steve and Dee, and an ongoing fruit of all four lives.

Why Christian Fellowship Is Needed

Christian fellowship is important to our ability to grow good fruit.

In I Peter 5:8 and 9, Peter warned us about our enemy. "Be self-controlled and alert. Your enemy the devil prowls around like a roaring lion looking for someone to devour. Resist him, standing firm in the faith, because you know that your brothers throughout the world are undergoing the same kind of sufferings."

Strong Christian support groups help keep our fruit from destruction when Satan attempts to block our efforts. He is the Christian's natural enemy, and as long as we are on this earth, we must deal with his underhanded and rarely blatant opposition.

In an attempt to conquer that which is threatening to conquer them, alcoholics have discovered the wisdom of looking for support from others who are fighting the same battle. The accountability factor is one reason "Alcoholics Anonymous" is such a successful program.

In one city where I lived, a group of people, all of whom have family members institutionalized for mental illness, have organized in an effort to find needed support. They get together at least once a month. One lady in that group told me, "I don't know what I would do if it were not for the support of those people." She added, "No one but those going through it understand."

Other Christians understand the battle we are fighting. They must deal with many of the same temptations and discouragements Satan uses against us. We can share with each other the shields which have been successful in our defense against Satan. We can receive encouragement from brothers and sisters who have been through it and have come out on top—or even why some failed. We can find the support that will enable us to grow stronger in following the Lord's will for our lives. As Ecclesiastes 4:9–10, and 12 remind us, "Two are better than one, because they have a good return for their work: If one falls down, his friend can help him up....Though one may be overpowered, two can defend themselves. A cord of three strands is not quickly broken."

Fruitfulness is also dependent on being in the proper environment. A plant must have the proper sunlight, soil, temperature, and water if it is to produce fruit. In the wrong environment, a plant will wither away long before it reaches the point of bearing fruit. We do not grow bananas in Ohio or maple trees in Southern California because the environment is wrong.

In II Corinthians 7:1 Paul instructs, "Since we have these promises, dear friends, let us purify ourselves from everything that contaminates body and spirit, perfecting holiness out of reverence for God."

The Christian must live in the world. We can be salt and light (Matthew 5:13-16) only when we are "rubbing shoulders" in this world. Christians cannot nor should they want to isolate themselves from non-Christians. But a controlled environment is important to our ability to produce Christ-honoring fruit.

Christian fellowship is the sunlight that causes the Christian to bloom. The warmth of that fellowship is the perfect temperature for developing healthy, fruit-producing Christians.

It is fellowship that allows us to focus on the proper role models.

I do not follow written instructions well. I once bought my children a gym set and decided to assemble it on my lunch hour. As it turned out, I spent the better part of the afternoon trying to figure out which was "bolt D," "bracket A," and "bar C." The instructions were more confusing than helpful to me. I finally ignored the instructions, and with the vow, "I will never buy another gym set as long as I live," I turned the last bolt.

While it is difficult for me to follow printed directions, I have no problem accomplishing a task which I have carefully watched someone demonstrate. I learn much quicker by seeing an example than by hearing or reading instructions.

The Bible includes instructions for living and serving, but it helps to see the Christian life demonstrated. Frank, making reference to a friend of his, told me, "I am a better man today because he *showed* me how to live."

Christian fellowship puts us in a position to see close-up the "ins and outs" of a fruit-bearing life. It gives us a firsthand opportunity to see how other, perhaps more mature, Christians handle difficult situations.

Very early in my Christian growth, I spent a lot of time with the young preacher who led me to the Lord. George Pevey took me to youth camps, rallies, revivals, and other activities. My presence at those events was extremely helpful to me; however, it was my exposure to that special man of God that challenged me the most. His most important contribution to my life was his demonstration of Christian living and service. George modeled Christianity for me. That was what I needed most to prepare the soil of my life for a harvest of godly fruit.

Paul wrote Titus about that very thing. He offered this challenge, "Similarly, encourage the young men to be self-controlled. In everything set them an example by doing what is good" (Titus 2:6-7).

No doubt Paul recognized the extremely important part a role model plays in Christian development, so he encouraged Titus to be the "model" for those with whom he would come in contact.

A word of caution is needed, though. We can be tempted to put our Christian "model" on a pedestal—and that is always a mistake. We can learn more from mature Christians when we allow them to be human and remember that they fail, too.

Essentials For Building Christian Fellowship

Logic dictates several considerations for building the kind of relationships that will bless, equip, and motivate us.

A good self-image is important to building relationships. As a young preacher, I did not build strong relationships with leaders of the church to which I was ministering. I became concerned about that situation, and desperately started looking for answers. The reason for that failure became obvious to me as I did some soul-searching. The problem was not with those leaders, but with me. I was afraid to be transparent. I was afraid those men would discover I wasn't all they thought me to be. They might even decide they did not want me to be their pastor if they knew me well. A poor self-image kept me from what could have been useful and satisfying relationships.

Even a brief look around reveals that each of us is unique. There are no two people alike. God made us that way in a wonderful diversity only He could create. He cared enough to personalize each of us. I saw a young man wearing a tee-shirt with bold letters across the front proclaiming, "God don't make no junk." I agree. The Master Craftsman created all people and He makes no mistakes; therefore, we do not have to be afraid to take off our masks.

Trust is another important consideration for building solid relationships. At the request of her husband, a young woman came to my office for counseling. Her husband had explained to me, "She refuses to let her guard down and get close to anyone, including me." He further stated, "People in the church have invited us into their homes, but she isn't interested."

The problem became obvious to me after only a few minutes with this troubled lady. She was deeply hurt during her childhood. Later, she suffered severe pain in a disappointing relationship with her first husband. She was afraid to trust again. The result was not only a shaky marriage, but also spiritual stagnation. She refused to get close to those who could help her move toward the kind of life that would glorify God.

To be fair, we must acknowledge that relationships involve a certain amount of risk; however, almost everything worthwhile involves risk. Surely the advantages of being a "people person" make the risk worthwhile. Taking chances is necessary for us to reach a place of maximum usefulness to the Lord. We can only reach others with the love of Christ as we allow ourselves to love.

Functioning at a reasonable pace is still another important consideration for building good relationships. A college professor gave me a valuable bit of advice early in my Christian life. He said, "Always make time for people, and let them know you have time for them."

A friend of mine asked a co-worker, "Is your wife still working part-time?" The man looked a bit puzzled and answered, "I don't know! A couple of months ago she was, but I have been so busy, we really have not talked for some time."

Undoubtedly, few men are so busy that they are unaware of their wife's employment status, but it is possible for us to become so busy that we do not have time to experience or nurture the joy of relationships. Relationships are much more likely to be pleasant and satisfying when life is slowed to a pace that allows for sensitivity to others.

How To Increase Fellowship Possibilities

Several steps may be taken to insure opportunities for fellowship.

We can plug into a small group in the church. Most churches have groups such as Sunday School classes, home Bible studies, choirs, ladies' groups, men's groups, discipleship groups, and, in some churches, sports teams and much more.

Participation in such groups usually provides opportunities to get into God's Word, to serve the Lord, and increases opportunities for fellowship. Fruitful living is greatly enhanced by seeking out a small group within the church family where involvement with God's people can be experienced on a more intimate level.

Betty, obviously a growing Christian, testified, "If I had not gone into that Sunday School class and gotten to know some of the people, I guess I would have gone through life missing much of what the Lord had for me."

We can be available to meet the needs of others. Real relationships grow out of attempts to meet the needs of the people around us. When a need is met in the life of someone, the recipient of the blessing will often become a friend to the person who met the need. Many of my closest friends first became my friends as a result of our mutual ministry to each other.

We can reflect a warm personality. That is not to say it is necessary to become a backslapping, joke telling, happy-go-lucky, life of the party type. It does mean a warm and genuine glow will result in people being drawn to us. That warmth comes from a Christ-like attitude.

I was impressed with John from the very first day I met him in a class we had together. There is nothing flashy about him. In fact, just the opposite is true. John is a rather quiet, soft-spoken person.

I enjoyed those qualities in him. I often sought him out for times of fellowship and sharing. I did not, at the time, try to evaluate what it was that caused me to like him. As I look back now, though, the reasons are not difficult to see. John always seemed to be smiling. He comes across as being real. He is what you see. He is a positive person.

Now that I think about it, many of the men in that

graduate program sought John out for bits of fellowship. I am sure they were drawn to him for the same reasons I was.

We can be responsive. Common sense tells us there are advantages to accepting the invitations that come our way. A young lady told me, "It's my fault no one ever asks me out anymore." She explained, "I used to get plenty of invitations, but I usually turned them down, so now no one bothers to ask anymore."

When a lady told me, "I have never felt a part of your church," I decided to find out why. My investigation revealed several people had tried to include her and her husband in various fellowships and activities, only to be rejected. When I confronted her with that information she responded, "They always asked me for times I did not have available, and, besides, no one has invited us to anything recently."

I do not doubt that no one has recently offered her an invitation because when people are turned down several times, they conclude that the people to whom they have been issuing invitations are not interested. Certainly it is worth some shuffling of schedules to open the door for fellowship with brothers and sisters in the Lord—fellowship that would enable us to move on toward the goal of glorifying God with our lives and serving Him as we serve others.

The Bottom Line

The bottom line is that people need encouragement. Encouragement cannot exist where there is no fellowship, improper fellowship, or surface relationships. Christians who are best equipped to make the right choices in a world dominated by Satan are those who take seriously the development of the right kind of relationships. They are those who work to break down barriers that would hinder relationships. They are those who remember that the first Christians devoted themselves to teaching *and* to fellowship (Acts 2:42).

PRINCIPLES TO PONDER:

1. Christian fellowship is vital in preparing the Christian to live and to serve effectively.

2. Christians need to identify and break down barriers that hinder fellowship.

3. Fellowship does not automatically happen. It requires initiative.

4. Involvement in the programs of the church is likely to create fellowship opportunities.

5. The Christian's actions can eliminate or create fellowship opportunities.

6. Encouragement is essential for us to become and remain spiritually productive.

PRACTICING THE PRINCIPLES:

1. List the small group fellowship opportunities your church offers. If you are not already involved in one or more of those opportunities, start visiting them in an effort to find which one(s) will best meet your fellowship needs.

2. Choose someone who is a new Christian or, perhaps, a stagnant Christian, with whom to initiate fellowship. Commit to develop that relationship indefinitely.

3. Survey the first six chapters of Acts, looking for the role of fellowship in the first-century church. Make notes on those chapters, comparing fellowship in the first-century church to fellowship in your church.

chapter seven

Choose the Right Balance

There are numerous reasons why the choice of a church home should be made with caution and much prayer. One reason is that a balanced church normally produces balanced Christians, while an unbalanced church is likely to produce unbalanced Christians. And not all churches are balanced. Some are concerned primarily with evangelism, but very little with the maturation of the believer. On the other hand, some churches have a "self" mentality, doing nothing to reach the lost. Some churches are known as Sunday School churches while others emphasize only worship. Doctrinal issues dominate some churches while others take the position that it doesn't matter what you believe. Social issues are big with many churches today while others completely ignore them.

It takes a portion of each of these to create a balanced church—one that reflects all of the same priorities Christ showed in His ministry on earth.

"Well-rounded" Christians are in the best position to grow the best fruit. For that reason, we need to stand ready to do whatever is necessary to stay balanced. Let us consider some balances essential for growing quality fruit.

Balance Between Building And Battling

"What is your opinion of those churches that insist upon taking an extreme position on social and political issues?" a young lady asked me.

Suspecting she wanted to express her own opinion, I asked, "What do you think?"

She replied, "I suppose it is good they are concerned about pornography, abortion, and other such issues, but I think they ought to be preaching the gospel! It is the gospel that will change the world."

She is absolutely right. It is the gospel that will change the world! But sometimes standing for one thing means standing against something else. And it is by what we stand for that others see the fruit of righteousness in us.

In Luke 14:28-33, Jesus uses two illustrations to teach would-be disciples to count the cost of entering into discipleship. He said that a man about to build a tower will first sit down and consider the cost. He also suggested a king going into battle will evaluate the situation before engaging enemy forces. Since Jesus mentions a builder and a battler, perhaps He is suggesting that discipleship involves both building and battling.

In the closing months of the Civil War, General Sherman marched through Georgia, burning almost everything in sight.

A man named John Schmitz fought under Sherman's command. After the war he returned to the south and settled in Adairsville, Georgia, my home town.

Mr. Schmitz first came to Georgia fighting for a cause in which he believed, but he returned as a builder. Mr. Schmitz, an architect, put his knowledge to work rebuilding what he had helped to destroy. He designed and built several major buildings in my home town, including my home church, which still stand today.

There is a time for building and a time for battling.

When Peter replied to Jesus, "You are the Christ, the Son of the living God," Jesus said to him, "...You are Peter, and on this rock I will build my church, and the gates of Hades will not overcome it" (Matthew 16:18).

How does this relate to the earlier illustrations? What does Christ mean? Gates can't attack!

That's right, but in this exchange, I see the picture of the church on the offensive—battering down the gates of hell. The Lord wants us to be battlers, but we are not to form wrecking crews.

Jesus expects us to be salt and light (Matthew 5:13-16), too. Salt preserves and adds flavor. Light shows the way. Christians are the builders of society, but we can't stamp out ungodly actions. We are most helpful when we replace them with positive action.

Balance Between Work And The Word

It happens often. Only the names and details change. Sam became a Christian, naturally excited about his new status and genuinely motivated by his newfound faith. Sam gladly accepted every new job offered to him at church. His enthusiasm knew no limits. After a short period of time, he agreed to teach a class of junior boys. He got involved in the weekly visitation program. He sang in the choir, took his turn at mowing the church lawn, and performed tasks too numerous to list. Everyone was thrilled with Sam. His growth was the talk of the church. "What this church needs is more Sams," several people proclaimed.

Then Sam's church attendance started to slip. He neglected some of his responsibilities. One Sunday he did not show up to teach the junior boys, neglecting to tell anyone that he needed a substitute. It was not long until Sam was seen back at the bar with the old gang, boozing it up. Shocked church members asked, "What happened to Sam? He was doing so well!"

Many Sams have appeared and then disappeared through the years. Too much responsibility too soon often results in "spiritual burnout." There was a lack of balance and Sam was overloaded.

How can we avoid spiritual casualties like Sam? We can be sure to maintain a balance between our devotional life and our Christian service. No one would deny that we are saved to serve, but we would be unwise to ignore the spiritual preparation that enables us to have a solid foundation for servanthood. Not even the Apostle Paul took over leadership roles immediately after he met the Lord. Instead, he became a student. First he studied with the disciples (Acts 9:19), then he went to Arabia for three years to grow in his faith (Galatians 1:18).

The other side of the coin is that we must not spend all our lives learning the Word, never giving any time for service. One preacher I know often talks about "spiritual porkers." He uses the term for those who feast at the trough of biblical knowledge without rendering any real service to the Lord.

The danger is that we will become so filled with head knowledge that we are of no earthly value to anyone, while viewing ourselves as spiritually superior to almost everyone else in the world. The study of God's Word must not be neglected. On the other hand, we must not fail to serve because all our time is used studying. The best results come to those who find a balance between the two.

Balance Between Secular And Christian Fellowship

"He is spending too much time with the wrong crowd." How many times has that statement been made about someone in a spiritual skid?

The other extreme is that we narrow our circle of friends to include only those who have already trusted the Lord, severely lessening the likelihood that we will ever lead anyone to Christ. How do we find a balance between fellowship with Christians and friendship with those outside the Lord? It's a tough question.

An automobile must visit a gas station for refueling. As we use up the gas in the tank, new fuel is required for it to keep operating. That is what Christian fellowship is—refueling. But an automobile that remains at the gas station all the time does no one any good. Sometimes Christians are content to remain at the fueling station of the church. How often does a car need to be refueled? That depends! Some cars get better mileage than others. More mature Christians may not need to spend as much time spiritually refueling with Christian fellowship as those less advanced. Those bits of fellowship that naturally come their way may be enough to carry them for longer times. The mature Christian can devote more time to building relationships that will enable him to be salt and light to the world.

The Apostle John warns about this involvement and the balance required.

> Do not love the world or anything in the world. If anyone loves the world, the love of the Father is not in him. For everything in the world—the cravings of sinful man, the lust of his eyes and the boasting of what he has and does—comes not from the Father but from the world. The world and its desires pass away, but the man who does the will of God live forever.
>
> (I John 2:15-17)

John is not suggesting that we shouldn't love the physical world, nor abstain from loving the people of this world. He is, however, warning us not to love the *world system* that opposes God, or the trinkets Satan dangles before us to make us take our eyes off Christ (Matthew 4:8-10). If we find our contact with non-Christian friends leading us toward affection for the world system, our balance probably is not right. We may need to spend more time at the *station* and less time on the *road.*

We can also go to the other extreme. We dare not allow fear of the world to keep us isolated from those who need Christ. The One who is in us is greater than the one who is in the world (I John 4:4). We do not have to be afraid of contact with the world, and we cannot afford to withdraw. We are God's ambassadors. The world needs what we have.

Balance Between Church And Family

A counselee's comment caught me a bit off guard one day. "I am starting to resent the church because it has taken my husband away from me," she declared.

When several wives expressed similar feelings to me over a six to eight month span, that caused me to evaluate some of our church programming and activities. I found a variety of activities such as building programs, athletic events, visitation, committee meetings, and other functions were tying up some men as frequently as five nights a week. It was obvious that over-involvement in church activities was contributing to the deterioration of some homes. I was crushed by what we had unknowingly done and became determined that I would not let it happen again.

However, there is a trap to be avoided at the other extreme. A preacher once asked me, "How do you find time to do any visitation?" He added, "On Sunday nights I am at church, and I must spend the other six nights with my family."

I explained to him that finding family time is a priority, and I constantly fight for that time, but I cannot do my job by spending six nights a week at home. We will over-compensate if we are not careful.

Our desire to accomplish the most with our lives demands that we find a balance between church responsibilities and family obligations. There are several realizations to be faced in attaining that balance.

Our first "ministry" obligation is to our own family. To a large degree, the success of the church is dependent on the success of the homes that make up that church. Strong family units make strong churches. When we invest time in our family, we are in reality investing that time in building the Lord's church.

Then, we may participate in church activities together with family members. The philosophy of most churches today seems to be that all church programming should be done by age group. A family of four may go to church together, but then go in four different directions when they arrive at the church doors. We need to find ways to be involved as a family even at church.

Sacrifice is also part of our relationship with the Lord. Giving a couple of nights a week to the Lord's work may necessitate sacrifice, but it surely does not constitute family neglect. We should be ready to sacrifice some personal time, while not shortchanging the family for which God also holds us accountable.

Family members should be consulted before we accept major church responsibilities, too. When family members share in the decision, they are more likely to be understanding and supportive. After all, the decision will affect each of them, too.

Adjustments should be made when circumstances change, too. With a baby on the way, the wife may not be able to continue with the same load of church responsibilities. Dad may have to work extra hours to send the kids through college, but when they graduate, he may have more time to give to church needs. Church responsibilities may have to be curtailed in times of family difficulties, but when things improve, it may be possible to give more attention to the programs of the church. It takes constant evaluation of our circumstances to find the best balance possible between family and church involvement.

But the family should not be used as an excuse for ignoring church work, and we should never use church work as an excuse for neglecting family activities. A spouse and children may grow to resent the church and the Lord if they think the church is robbing them of time with their husband or father. Conversely, if the family is not shown, by our involvement in the church, that it is worthy of support, they are not likely to ever hold the church in very high regard.

In homes where a husband or wife is more advanced spiritually than the spouse, it is especially important to find the right balance between church and family. Otherwise, unwholesome friction is likely to become a way of life. A weaker mate cannot be led to become stronger by a spouse with little commitment to the Lord's work, while he is likely to be turned off to the church by a mate who gives every spare minute to the church.

What constitutes balance between family and church will change with growth and circumstances. No one can tell us how much time should be devoted to each. We must be sensitive to changes and discover what is the proper balance for us. Then we are more likely to be genuinely useful, fruitful, and effective.

Balance Between Faith And Logic

Everyone who has served on a church board has heard it, only the names and details change. After a proposal is made, Brother Fred explains, "That all sounds good, but we just cannot afford it now. We will have to wait a few years until we build up our bank account a bit."

Then Brother Charlie is given the floor to offer his rebuttal. "The Lord blesses faith," he says, "not sight. Let's not be concerned with money. After all, our Father owns the cattle on a thousand hills."

So where do we draw the line between faith and logic? This is a question we struggle with in our personal lives as well as in church-wide decisions. The answer is vital to our ability to be used effectively for the Lord.

David told me, "I believe it is God's will for me to relocate and change jobs." He went on to say, "The problem is that to do so will be quite a financial sacrifice and I have my family to think about." He was torn between doing the logical thing, which was to remain in his present position, and doing what he felt God wanted him to do, which was to move. A move at that time would require a strong faith.

"Is my faith too weak?" he asked.

I responded with one question for David. "Are you sure it is God's will for you to relocate?" I explained to him, "Refusal to be in God's will because of fear indicates a lack of faith, but if you are not convinced such a move is God's will, you would be foolish to change your current status."

David was convinced it was God's will and explained to me why he was convinced. David took the new position and the move worked out beautifully. God has provided wonderfully for David and his family.

The question of faith or logic often boils down to a question of God's will. When an action is God's will, we are smart to go for it! God will provide. If there is doubt about whether God has given a go-ahead, we would be foolish to act. To buy a large and beautiful house, expecting God to provide the money miraculously to pay for it would be totally out of line…unless God has honestly revealed to us in some definite way that it is His will. Then it would be foolish not to buy it. If it is His will, He will provide a way.

We may wonder, "But how do I determine the will of God?" Volumes have been written on the subject. We'll leave it here with only two basic suggestions. (1) In seeking God's will, we are wise to consult the Bible first. God's will can most often be determined by the principles found there. (2) We should pray for God's guidance. God will let us know in some way if He has a preference, but there may be times when God does not have a preference.

A preacher received a call away from a small struggling church to a large, thriving metropolitan congregation. Excitedly he said to his wife, "Honey, I'm going upstairs to pray and seek God's will, in the meantime you start packing." This approach lacks more than genuine sincerity! Prayer is more than a routine we go through to satisfy God. We must be honestly receptive to His directions.

Avoid Fanaticism

We have discussed a few of the balances necessary for the Christian to be fruitful. There are others. Our desire to grow the fruit of righteousness in our lives and homes will cause us to guard against unbiblical extremes which may constitute fanaticism.

Once, years ago, my youngest daughter Sandy and I got on a teeter-totter at the school playground. Since she was, at that time, about one-third my size, what happened was predictable. She went up in the air, I went to the ground, and that's the way we remained until I got off. Movement was halted because of imbalance, an essential to the movement of a teeter-totter.

For the Christian's continued usefulness as a producer of the fruit of righteousness, balance is also essential. Imbalance halts our growth.

PRINCIPLES TO PONDER:

1. It takes balanced churches to produce balanced Christians.

2. There is a sense in which Christians are to be both builders and battlers.

3. We grow stronger in our ability to serve as we grow stronger in our knowledge of God's Word.

4. When we allow the Holy Spirit to dominate our lives, we do not have to fear being negatively influenced by those outside Christ.

5. Families are the smaller units of which the church is composed.

6. God's will is the factor that transforms what seems to be foolishness into faith.

PRACTICING THE PRINCIPLES:

1. Ask your closest Christian friends to help you determine if there is imbalance in any area of your life. Make adjustments where adjustments are needed, asking the Lord for His help.

2. Have a family conference in which you discuss *church time* versus *family time*. Schedule both to the satisfaction of all family members and in keeping with the principles in Scripture.

3. Study the Sermon on the Mount (Matthew 5, 6, 7), listing appropriate balances mentioned or implied.

chapter eight

Choose the Right Schedule

Much of Edie's time is occupied with being a wife and mother of two. However, she also works an eight hour a day job outside the home. She once told me, "I am frustrated by my lack of time for church activities. It is impossible for me to find the time necessary to build solid relationships."

Edie's dilemma is one multitudes of Christians face. I hear many sincere people make statements like, "I would love to get involved, but I just don't have the time." In fact, I have often made that statement myself.

But what do we mean when we say, "I don't have the time?"

If we mean time is not available to us for unimportant activities because it is being used for important endeavors, then we are certainly making a valid statement. If we mean, we don't have time for the important matters, because we have committed our time to things that do not matter much, then we may need to reevaluate our commitments and priorities.

Paul wrote to the Ephesians, "Be very careful, then, how you live—not as unwise but as wise, making the most of every opportunity, because the days are evil" (5:15-16). The needs in our world dictate that we take seriously the disbursement of our allotted twenty-four hours a day. Wise management of time is nothing more than making the most of every opportunity.

Right Priorities Are Important

All of us have twenty-four hours in each day and seven days in each week. The challenge is to use that time with the least amount of waste.

Circumstances may force us into certain time molds, and that is as it should be. For example, it is right that a man give time to supporting himself and his family. In I Timothy 5:8, Paul wrote, "If anyone does not provide for his relatives, and especially for his immediate family, he has denied the faith and is worse than an unbeliever." Paul wrote to the Thessalonians, "Make it your ambition to lead a quiet life, to mind your own business and to work with your hands, just as we told you, so that your daily life may win the respect of outsiders and so that you will not be dependent on anybody" (I Thessalonians 4:11-12).

My two daughters, through the years, kept my wife busy at times running a taxi service to and from basketball practice, volleyball, track, piano lessons, Girl Scouts, bowling, and much more. It is not unusual for mothers (and fathers) to find themselves forced into time molds created by their children's interests as well as other circumstances.

The fact remains, however, that most of us generally decide how a good portion of our time will be used. "Making the most of every opportunity" comes down to keeping priorities in order.

God created time and He created man. Therefore, it is reasonable that God, the Creator, should have a voice in how we use our time. There are certain actions God expects of us. These expectations are not optional.

For example, God instructs us to worship with other Christians and encourage them (Hebrews 10:25); to pray (I Thessalonians 5:17, James 5:16); to make disciples (Matthew 28:19), and a number of others things which require a portion of our time. Priorities are best set with an open Bible in one hand. It is right to schedule everything else around that which God requires of us. The trap to avoid is that of investing our time in activities which have no bearing on eternity for us or for others.

An occasional time study is often helpful, too. Keeping records of how we use our time for a particular period enables us to discover what we see as priorities. A time study may reveal to us that our priorities are different than we thought. That does not mean no time should be taken for recreation, hobbies, and relaxation, but God does require that certain activities be in our schedules. We are wise to honor His expectations first (Proverbs 1:7). He knows best what we need, and we can be sure of that when we give undivided attention to God's stated guidelines.

Most people distribute their time on the basis of their personal priorities. But it is when we identify and pursue the important ones that we can expect to make a real difference.

For instance, I enjoy sports. I have been on football,

basketball, baseball, track, and softball teams. I enjoy few things more than a round of golf. Sports can be worthwhile, but we dare not allow them to keep us from serving the Lord.

Clubs and community organizations are often worthwhile and our involvement needed. But they may or may not deserve a top spot on our list of priorities.

Vocational advancement is a worthy pursuit, but it is possible for ambition to get in the way of our call to discipleship.

It is possible to love God and at the same time lose blessings He wants us to have. That can happen when we don't love Him *most*. Jesus said, "Your heavenly Father knows that you need them. But seek first his kingdom and his righteousness" (Matthew 6:33). The best fruit is produced when we seek His kingdom and righteousness *first*.

Getting and keeping priorities straight is a key to using time wisely, but it is possible to have our priorities straight and still fail. That can happen if we do not practice sound principles for making the most of our time.

Time Is Most Valuable When Organized

Unfortunately, complaining about a time shortage does not give us more time. It is those who organize their time who get the most out of each day. Here are several suggestions that will help us get the most out of our twenty-four hours.

Spending time each day with God is bound to help. We need God's help to get the most out of each day He gives us. Spending some time with God early in the day enables us to put things in the proper perspective. It gives us strength to accomplish the maximum in each day. One man whom I highly respect told me, "Spending forty-five minutes with

God early in the morning doubles my productivity in that day."

Another person said, "If I don't spend some time with God in the morning, I end up running around most of the day like a person who doesn't know where he is going." Some time with God each day gives us purpose and direction.

Organizing time on a weekly basis will be helpful. I divide each day of the week into three slots—morning, afternoon, and evening. On Monday morning I put all my anticipated activities for the week into those twenty-one slots. I often schedule the most difficult jobs early in the week, so as to eliminate possible anxiety because I'm anticipating them. My plan for the week is often interrupted, but that's okay, because there is usually room for flexibility in my schedule.

Planning the week helps in a number of ways. It eliminates wasted time involved in jumping from one job to another and then back again. It also cuts down on time used in trying to decide what to do next. Most of all, it eliminates anxiety, enabling us to feel on top of things. That in itself adds significantly to our ability to do the most for the Lord.

Time management experts tell us we should plan to do the jobs that require the greatest mental effort at the times when we are at our mental peak. For most people that will be in the morning. These precious hours should not be wasted with jobs that can be performed at times when our minds are less than sharp. For example, as a pastor, I do not do regular hospital visitation (except when surgery is scheduled) and routine administration during the morning hours. That would be a misuse of my time. Those responsibilities can easily be taken care of in the afternoon. The mornings are reserved for study. This practice enables me to get the most out of my study time, and thus cut down on the number of hours needed for sermon preparation.

We can also get more out of our time by eliminating wasted motion. We do that by arranging our schedule so as to cut down on time required for going from one task to another. For example, instead of going for groceries in the morning, a housewife might wait until her son has finished basketball practice and stop by the supermarket when she goes to retrieve him from the gymnasium. A few minutes are saved because she makes one trip instead of two.

Keeping good records can also save us time. Early in my ministry I discovered certain advantages to keeping files for every program and event I plan. Now when I plan an event, I save valuable time by going to files from previous programs. I am not faced with the ominous task of starting from scratch each time.

When we organize personal papers properly, we do not lose valuable time looking for them later when they are needed. It is profitable to make notes from our study of God's Word and systematically file those notes. This practice cuts down on research when we come back to that passage to prepare for a devotional or Bible lessons. An adequate filing system makes it possible for us to draw successfully from our past efforts.

We can make the most of our time by using small blocks of time that are traditionally wasted. Are there fifteen more minutes a day we can use for the Lord? If so, we have gained ninety hours a year. That is more than two work weeks.

One day while eating lunch alone, I became a little ashamed of myself when I noticed a man at a nearby table reading the Bible as he ate. I was reading a newspaper. Perhaps it's impossible to use your lunch hour for anything but eating, but what about the ride home from work (if you are not driving)? Could that time be used constructively? Maybe time spent in the waiting area of the doctor's office could be put to good use. Could we make better use of our break time? There is lost time in most of our lives, time that could be used.

Learning to sometimes say "no" may be a step in the right direction. Almost everyone in today's fast moving society must contend with unrealistic demands on their time. All of us have seen the World War II military recruiting posters depicting Uncle Sam all dressed up in red, white, and blue pointing straight at us with the caption "Uncle Sam Wants You." Like Uncle Sam, many people have the idea they cannot do without us. Our concern for making the most of our days makes it necessary for us to evaluate all those demands carefully—and say "no" to some.

Our egos may be the factor that make it difficult for us to turn down invitations to serve on boards or get involved in community functions; however, many of those functions can be successful without us. That doesn't mean we should abstain from all involvement, but we must be careful not to overschedule. We may have to say "no" to some extremely worthy causes. We all have twenty-four hours a day, but there are only so many things that can be done in twenty-four hours.

Building on the work of others is still another way to save time. A speaker I once heard said, "I know a man who said, 'I will be original or nothing,' sure enough that's what he is, *nothing!*" The same speaker humorously stated, "I am convinced, after my death, they will hang my portrait over the copier machine at my alma mater as a memorial to me."

Plagiarism certainly is not acceptable, but building on

the foundation of knowledge discovered and recorded by others is good common sense. I learned that lesson when I was a student working on a college maintenance crew. My supervisor was hospitalized for several weeks one summer. Without the supervision of our boss, my partner and I were often faced with the challenge of doing jobs in which we had little experience or expertise; however, we had a friend who worked at the local lumber yard who was a "jack of all trades." We often went to Mr. Clark for advice about jobs of which we knew very little, rather than fumbling through them on our own. Our friend at the lumber yard saved us many frustrating hours of labor that summer.

Caution Advised

Ted Engstrom often tells a story during his seminars that may help put time management in the proper perspective.

Bob attended a time management seminar and came back excited about putting what he had learned to work. He bought a stopwatch, and used it, among other things, to time his wife as she made breakfast. Afterward he announced to her, "Honey, you took eight and one-half minutes to prepare breakfast. I can show you how to do it in six minutes." The good news is that breakfast is now being cooked in six minutes! The bad news is that Bob is now doing the cooking.

It is possible to become so rigid with time management that we offend some people. Poor relationships can only hinder our efforts. That might be one of the things Paul had in mind when he wrote to the Colossians, "Walk in wisdom toward them that are without, redeeming the time" (4:5, KJV).

Use It Wisely

Let us suppose that we put to work in our lives some principles that enable us to have some extra time. Now the question is, "What will we do with that time?"

A man worked for years, putting a little money aside with each pay check. One day he went to the bank and withdrew every cent. Within a week he spent his life savings, and had nothing to show for it. "Why did you do such a thing?" a friend asked with a tone of disbelief.

A bit irritated, he answered, "It was mine, and I had the right to do what I wanted with it."

Do we feel the time we save is ours to use however we choose? Most of us want to invest it in that which will be permanent. Do we filter our "extra" time through the poet's test: "Only one life, It soon will be past. Only what is done for Christ will last."

"The main thing is to keep the main thing the main thing." I would give credit if I knew to whom to attribute that quotation, but regardless of who said it, it sounds like good advice for those of us who would effectively serve our Lord.

PRINCIPLES TO PONDER:

1. We all have twenty-four hours a day and seven days a week.

2. The challenge in managing our time is to use it with the least amount of waste.

3. We will distribute our time in accordance with our priorities.

4. Priorities should be determined in light of the principles and commandments of God's Word.

5. We get the most out of our time when it is organized.

6. Correct time management takes relationships into consideration.

PRACTICING THE PRINCIPLES:

1. List what you believe to be the three most important priorities of the Christian, supporting each with a Scripture reference.

2. Evaluate the use of your time by keeping a detailed account of how you use it for an entire week. Then make the proper adjustments.

3. Read Matthew 12—16, jotting down everything that comes to mind about Jesus' use of time in this section of Scripture.

chapter nine

Choose to Cultivate the Right Integrity

"I don't care what people think!" A somewhat provoked young man blurted this out when, at his father's request, I attempted to explain to him some of the negative consequences that his involvement in certain questionable activities was sure to have on his work for the Lord. "I am obligated to please God and God alone," he declared.

Must we be concerned with what people think? After all, when Peter and the other apostles were warned by the Sanhedrin to stop teaching in the name of Jesus, they ignored the admonition and proceeded to fill Jerusalem with their teaching. They responded to a reprimand by declaring, "We must obey God rather than men!" (Acts 5:29).

Didn't Joshua call upon the people of his day to make

a decision as to where they would place their loyalty? Joshua's statement left no doubt about where he stood, "As for me and my household," he said, "we will serve the Lord" (Joshua 24:15).

Most of us who have suffered the futility and frustration of attempting to please everyone who makes demands of us would concur with the observation Herbert Bayard Swope voiced at a testimonial dinner in his honor. "I cannot give you the formula for success," he said, "but I can give you formula for failure—try to please everyone."

No clear-minded Christian would question that his first allegiance is to God. Logic and Scripture demand that discrepancies between the expectations of God and man can only be dealt with satisfactorily by yielding to God. Most of us would agree there are no legitimate reasons to compromise that principle.

Does that mean we never need to be concerned about our earthly image? No, it does not! The Christian is primarily concerned with pleasing God, but it is to His advantage for us to maintain the respect of the people around us. While it is a mistake to compromise God's will to please people, we would do well to remember that *respect* is almost sure to add to our ability to accomplish something good for God. Respect opens doors, giving us opportunities that otherwise would be lost and opens doors to receive support for our endeavors.

Salt and Light

We often refer to Jesus' instructions before His ascension—those recorded in Matthew 28:19-20—as "the great commission," but the charge Jesus gave His disciples almost three years earlier may be the more complete statement of the Christian's reason for being. This doesn't minimize His mandate to go into the world teaching and baptizing, because the earlier assignment actually incorporated those elements into its implementation.

Sitting with His disciples on a quiet Galilean hillside Jesus instructed:

> You are the salt of the earth. But if the salt loses its saltiness, how can it be made salty again? It is no longer good for anything, except to be thrown out and trampled by men. You are the light of the world. A city on a hill cannot be hidden. Neither do people light a lamp and put it under a bowl. Instead they put it on its stand, and it gives light to everyone in the house. In the same way, let your light shine before men that they may see your good deeds and praise your Father in Heaven.
>
> (Matthew 5:13-16)

Everyone knows salt seasons food. But before the days of refrigeration, it was also used as a preservative. Meat was salted to protect it from spoilage.

Light serves a series of vastly important functions. For one thing, it allows us to see in the day or in dark places. It enables us to find our way. Life without light would be difficult at best. Studies have shown that light deprivation can cause illness or depression.

Like salt and light, disciples of Jesus have purpose and usefulness. A professor friend of mine used to say, "Christians are not only good, they are good for something." Jesus instructed His disciples to guard against losing their "saltiness." Tasteless salt benefits no one.

In eastern countries in the time of Jesus, salt was impure or mingled with vegetable substances. It was possible for it to lose its saltiness while a considerable quantity of matter remained. Sometimes after losing its "saltiness," salt was thrown like gravel on paths or roads and trampled into the dirt.

Jesus also instructed that we are not to hide our lights under a cover. The world needs lighthouses to direct it away from disaster and to the safety of a life in Christ. "The god of this age has blinded the minds of unbelievers, so that they cannot see the light of the gospel of the glory of Christ....For God who said, 'Let light shine out of darkness,' made his light shine in our hearts to give us the light of the knowledge of the glory of God in the face of Christ" (II Corinthians 4:4,6).

By retaining our "saltiness" and keeping our lights shining, we maintain the credibility that enables us to be in a position to influence our world.

People need to see the light of Christ in us so they will be drawn to the Light Source and motivated to glorify the Father in heaven. Our ability to be lighthouses for Christ is closely tied to our desire to glorify God. A Sunday School teacher remarked to me concerning a well-mannered new child in her class, "I am looking forward to meeting his parents. I know by the child's behavior they are special people."

People may be extremely anxious to know our Father when they conclude that we are delightfully different because He has changed our lives.

Ambassadors

We are ambassadors of Christ, representing Him on this earth. As ambassadors of Christ, we are expected to act appropriately in order to elevate people's perception of *Him*.

We are responsible to maintain our own credibility to affirm the credibility of the one we represent. It's part of the job description.

A young Christian who had made a serious mistake spoke repentantly to me through his tears. "What concerns me most about this," he said, "is not what people will think of me, but what they will think of my Lord." He recognized his role as Christ's ambassador and regretted the fact that by compromising his own integrity, he let the Lord down.

I remember singing an old hymn, "I Am A Stranger Here," in the services of the little country church where I worshiped as a child. It proclaimed, "I am a stranger here, within a foreign land: my home is far away, upon a golden strand; ambassadors to be of realms beyond the sea, I'm here on business for my king."

Could there by any higher reason for guarding our integrity? Our business is the King's business.

Scriptural Encouragement

A number of New Testament passages emphatically exhort believers to keep their work alive by living beyond reproach. Let's consider several of those passages.

In I Timothy 4:12-14, Paul instructs his young son in the faith to set an example in speech, in life, in love, in faith, and in purity. Timothy is told to devote his time to ministry. Then in verses 15 and 16 the apostle pleads, "Be diligent in these matters; give yourself wholly to them, so that everyone may see your progress. Watch your life and doctrine closely. Persevere in them, because if you do, you will save both yourself and your hearers."

Peter wrote similar instructions. "Dear friends, I urge you, as aliens and strangers in the world, to abstain from sinful desires, which war against your soul. Live such good lives among the pagans that, though they accuse you of doing wrong, they may see your good deeds and glorify God on the day he visits us" (I Peter 2:11-12).

Peter even suggests unbelieving husbands can be drawn to the Lord when wives behave with purity and reverence. He adds that development of inner beauty and a gentle and quiet spirit will greatly aid the ability of the wife to point her husband to the Lord (I Peter 3:1-6).

These Scriptures and others like them reveal that God expects believers to protect their saltiness, their brightness, and the effectiveness of their ambassadorship with a superior reputation.

Ida Kays says it well in a thought-provoking poem entitled "Powerless."

> Once I bought my son an engine
>   That would circle 'round and 'round,
> For I knew he'd be so happy
>   When his 'lectric train he found.
>
> Like a boy, myself, I set it
>   Going 'neath the Christmas tree—
> All my dignity forgotten
>   As I watched in childish glee.
>
> Then it stopped, I tried to mend it,
>   Turned it here and punched it there,
> But my knowledge of mechanics
>   Found no trouble anywhere.

I was disappointed sorely—
    As I knew the boy would be.
Then I spied a glittering something
    That had fallen from the tree.

Surely that wee bit of tinsel
    On the rail no harm had done,
But I brushed it off—and presto—
    How that train began to run!

But my smile of joy soon faded
    As I slowly turned the key.
Through that incident of playtime,
    What a lesson came to me!

Oh, how many lives are useless—
    Standing still, or sliding back!
Something foreign cuts the current—
    Maybe tinsel on the track.

Just a bit of something shiny,
    Something harmless in its place,
But it makes all effort fruitless,
    There's no power for the race.

Track is smooth and train is ready,
    The machinery has no lack;
You alone, can find the trouble—
    Get the tinsel off the track!

Then again, your train goes speeding
    On the round the Master Hand
Laid before you—on the mission
    That His love and wisdom planned![1]

Foundational Credibility Factors

Let's consider four factors paramount to maintaining spiritual credibility.

Factor #1—Spiritual credibility is maintained by the integrity of a pure life. Paul wrote to Timothy about this principle:

> In a large house there are articles not only of gold and silver, but also of wood and clay; some are for noble purposes and some for ignoble. If a man cleanses himself from the latter, he will be an instrument for noble purposes, made holy, useful to the Master and prepared to do any good work.
>
> (II Timothy 2:20-21)

The writer likens the believer to dishes. Some dishes are decorative and adorn the table beautifully when guests are present. Others serve well back in the kitchen, but all the dishes must first be clean to be useful. It is equally true that some Christians are extremely visible vessels, while others work behind the scenes, but all must be clean to be useful.

I encourage young men to pursue the ministry, but Ted (not his real name) was different. He possessed a combination of ministry gifts rarely distributed to one individual. Besides that, he was a man with a heart for people. All the needed ingredients seemed to be in place, and I predicted he would someday be one of the most effective ministers of the gospel in our nation. He was well on his way when it happened. Ted yielded to the flesh!

Of course, Ted lost his position with the church, but he lost exceedingly more than that. Yes, the Lord forgives when we ask out of a repentant heart to be forgiven (I John 1:9), but an act of immorality forever limited the ministry of that young man who had unlimited potential.

Such tragedies are certainly not confined to "professional clergy." The sad fact is, it only takes the *perception* of immorality to devastate one's spiritual effectiveness. My mentor in the faith warned me only months after I accepted the Lord, "You do not have to fall to void your witness, people only have to believe you have fallen." Caution is certainly in order.

Factor #2—Spiritual credibility is maintained by the integrity of one's endeavors. There are three components to our endeavors that are most likely to be viewed with interest.

1. The *identities* of our endeavors may come under close scrutiny.

The letter was worded similar to others I received from representatives of churches and groups where I am scheduled to speak. "...We are excited about having you as our guest speaker for the week of special meetings. Would you please provide us with biographical information? Be sure to include the names of service clubs in which you hold membership as well as boards and committees on which you sit."

The writer obviously anticipated that awareness of such information would enhance my credibility in the eyes of the people to whom I would speak. People are interested in the enterprises in which we choose to invest our lives.

2. The *energy* expended on our chosen endeavors also comes under consideration.

The world is not impressed as much by our involvement in various ventures as by the zeal and energy with which we approach those projects. Hard work wins respect. The American work ethic is a great part of our national heritage. Our credibility is elevated when we adhere to it.

3. The *methods* chosen to pursue our endeavors are crucial to the integrity of those endeavors—and rightly so. Scripture instructs, "…Whatever you do, do it all for the glory of God. Do not cause anyone to stumble" (I Corinthians 10:31-32). A godly approach to worthy endeavors honors God and lends credibility to our work.

Factor #3—Spiritual credibility is maintained by the integrity of a proper spirit.

A lady, making reference to a speaker we all heard the previous evening, asked, "Wasn't he a gifted speaker?"

"Yes," answered one of our group, "but I didn't like his attitude much."

That speaker's effort was wasted on some of us because he had a poor spirit. On the other hand, a good attitude may compensate for a multitude of weaknesses. I heard it said of a Sunday School teacher, "He is not especially gifted, nor particularly innovative, but he is effective because he has such a sweet spirit."

Factor #4—Spiritual credibility is maintained by the integrity of pure motives. At one time or another most of us have heard such accusations as, "He's just in it for what he can get out of it," or "All she is interested in is the prestige." The ability to represent our Lord well can be weakened or strengthened by how our motives are perceived. It is a fact that people often look beyond our actions, attempting to discern the reasons for those actions. Those conclusions are mentally computed as a prime consideration when credibility factors are being evaluated.

The writer of Hebrews wrote of having a clear conscience

and living honorably in every way (Hebrews 13:18). That is always the goal for those who are concerned with growing the fruit of righteousness.

FOOTNOTE

[1]Taken from *Out of My Treasures*, Vol. 1, p. 172, College Press, 1962.

PRINCIPLES TO PONDER:

1. We are obligated to please God *first*.

2. Integrity enables Christians to retain their "saltiness" and keep their "lights" bright.

3. The Christian's chief concern in this world is the Lord's business.

4. Scripture teaches us that we keep our work vibrant by living beyond reproach.

5. Only clean vessels are useful.

6. Integrity is affected as certainly by the motivation for the action as by the action itself.

PRACTICING THE PRINCIPLES:

1. Rate yourself on a scale of one to ten in regard to each of the four "foundational credibility factors." Ask a family member also to rate you and then discuss any differences in the ratings.

2. Identify the endeavors where you are displaying the poorest spirit and pray specifically that God will help you improve your spirit in those areas where you are struggling most.

3. List the fruit of the Spirit from Galatians 5:22-23 and write one sentence about each, explaining how the presence or absence of that particular fruit can enhance or hinder your integrity.

chapter ten

Choose the Right Assistance

Two wives sat mending their husbands' pants. One of the ladies said to the other, "My poor Charlie is totally discouraged with his church work. He told me he is considering resigning his leadership position. It seems that nothing is going right for him."

The other lady, somewhat perplexed, replied, "Why, that is odd. My John is saying just the opposite. He is excited about his work for the Lord, and it seems he is closer to the Lord than ever before."

That is the direction the conversation took as they continued mending the trousers, one patching the *knees* and the other the *seat.*

It is not difficult to figure out which wife was patching the seat and which was patching the knees. A healthy prayer life is often the major difference between a fruitful life and one of spiritual stagnation.

Someone said, "It's a real coincidence that when I pray, good things happen, but when I do not, life seems to go sour."

That, of course, is no coincidence. Paul wrote, "Do not be anxious about anything, but in everything, by prayer and petition, with thanksgiving, present your requests to God. And the peace of God, which transcends all understanding, will guard your hearts and your minds in Christ Jesus" (Philippians 4:6-7).

Those who know where to go for help accomplish the most in this world. Attaining that help, though, requires an understanding of how to approach God.

Principles For Approaching God
Prayer that helps us most is unceasing prayer.

A now defunct publication called *Wonderful Word* once published a story that helped me understand what it means to pray unceasingly.

A number of ministers were assembled for the discussion of different questions, and among others one question asked was how a person could comply with the command to "pray without ceasing" (I Thessalonians 5:17). Various suppositions were stated, and at length one of the group was appointed to write an essay on it to be read at the next meeting. This was overheard by a female servant. She exclaimed, "What! A whole month wanted to tell the meaning of that text! It is one of the easiest and best texts in the Bible."

"Well, well," said an old minister, "Mary, what can you say about it? Let us know how you understand it. Can you pray all the time?"

"Oh, yes, sir."

"What! When you have so many things to do?"

"Why, sir, the more I have to do the more I can pray."

"Indeed! Well, Mary, do let us know how it is, for most people think otherwise."

"Well, sir," said the girl, "when I first open my eyes in the morning, I pray, 'Lord, open the eyes of my understanding; and while I am dressing, I pray that I may be clothed with the robe of righteousness....As I begin work, I pray that I may have strength equal to my day. When I begin to kindle up a fire, I pray that God's Word may revive in my soul; and as I sweep out the house, I pray that my heart may be cleansed from all its impurities. While preparing and partaking of breakfast, I desire to be fed with the sincere milk of the Word! As I am busy with the little children, I look up to God as my Father, and pray for the spirit of adoption, that I may show others that I am His child, and so on all day. Everything I do furnishes me with a thought for prayer."

Does *everything* we do furnish us with thought for prayer?

Prayer means the most to our lives when it is a natural part of living. Unceasing prayer keeps us strong and challenged—branches of the vine capable of maximum fruit production.

Prayer helps us most when backed by faith.

Faith is to prayer what an engine is to an automobile. A car is most useful when it has a motor. Prayer benefits us when it is paired with faith...believing that God will do what is best for us.

Once, when Jesus and His disciples were outside the little village of Bethany, He said to a fig tree, "May you never bear fruit again!" (Matthew 21:19). Later, when they returned to that spot, Peter was stunned to see that the tree had withered. In response to Peter's surprise, Jesus said:

> "Have faith in God....I tell you the truth, if anyone says to this mountain, 'Go, throw yourself into the sea,' and does not doubt in his heart but believes that what he says will happen, it will be done for him. Therefore I tell you, whatever you ask for in prayer, believe that you have received it, and it will be yours."
>
> (Mark 11:22-24)

The writer of Hebrews also writes about the part faith plays in prayer. "And without faith it is impossible to please God, because anyone who comes to him must believe that he exists and that he rewards those who earnestly seek him" (11:6).

Prayer helps us most when offered out of a forgiving heart.

In a counseling session, Jan told me, "My prayers are not being answered." She was concerned that her efforts seemed to be fruitless, and her spiritual life was in a tailspin.

I questioned Jan in an effort to find the reason for the failure she saw in her prayer life. After inquiring about her faith, the purity of her life, her prayer habits, and several other factors critical to successful prayer, I asked, "What about your feelings toward others? Are you harboring any bitterness in your heart toward anyone?"

There was a long silence and then tears began to fill her eyes. "That may be the problem," she said quietly. Jan then confessed to me that she had bitter feelings toward a sister in Christ.

I encouraged her to go to that sister and work things out. After I prayed with her, she left my office, assuring me she would take care of it immediately. A few days later I received a note from her that simply stated, "I did what you suggested, and my prayers are being answered again. Praise God!"

Jesus told us, "And when you stand praying, if you hold anything against anyone, forgive him, so that your Father in heaven may forgive you your sins" (Mark 11:25).

Prayer offered out of a forgiving heart is the kind of prayer to which God responds. We are strong and fit for service to God when our hearts are free of bitterness and open to Christ-like attitudes.

Prayer benefits us most when offered unselfishly.

James accused, "When you ask, you do not receive, because you ask with wrong motives, that you may spend what you get on your pleasures" (4:3).

James did not mean to suggest that we should never ask anything for ourselves. His point is that it is inappropriate to make requests of God that are motivated strictly by desire for pleasure. Prayer that is *pleasure centered* can never be *power packed*.

Prayer benefits us most when offered in Jesus' name.

Jesus said, "I will do whatever you ask in my name, so that the Son may bring glory to the Father. You may ask me for anything in my name, and I will do it" (John 14:13-14).

Later, He said to His disciples, "I tell you the truth, my Father will give you whatever you ask in my name. Until now you have not asked for anything in my name. Ask and you will receive, and your joy will be complete" (John 16:23-24).

To ask in the name of Jesus can mean three things.

First, it means to ask as a representative of Jesus. We are His ambassadors (II Corinthians 5:20). When we ask anything of God the Father, it should be on behalf of Christ the Son.

Second, to ask in the name of Jesus means to ask by the authority of Jesus. Prayer offered in the name of Jesus demands attention that could not otherwise be demanded. Scripture says, "Therefore God exalted him to the highest place and gave him the name that is above every name" (Philippians 2:9). It's no wonder that prayers offered in the name of Jesus carry weight in heaven.

Third, to pray in the name of Jesus means to acknowledge Him as the bridge whereby we have access to the Father. Jesus is our mediator (Hebrews 8:6, 9:15, 12:24). As our mediator, He guarantees our access to God the Father. We do not have to go to God on the basis of our own merit when we pray in Jesus' name.

Prayer benefits us most when offered in an attitude of humility.

Two men were praying in the temple. One was a Pharisee and the other a tax collector. In those days you could not get much more religious than a Pharisee, while tax collectors were the scum of the earth in the eyes of the Jews.

The Pharisee stood before God telling Him of his own good deeds, thanking God that he was not a sinner like the tax collector. The tax collector, on the other hand, did not consider himself worthy to look to heaven, but beat his breast, and said, "God, have mercy on me, a sinner."

Jesus said it was the tax collector and not the Pharisee who went home justified before God. Why? "For everyone who exalts himself will be humbled, and he who humbles himself will be exalted" (Luke 18:9-14).

The Bible tells us that, "God opposes the proud but gives grace to the humble" (Proverbs 3:34; I Peter 5:5).

Perhaps the best way to attain humbleness is to focus on the greatness of God. It is difficult to see ourselves greater than we are while focusing on the majesty of God.

Principles For Organizing A Quiet Time

It is a wise Christian who regularly sets aside time to be with God. In recent years the phrase "quiet time" has been used to describe that regular time of sharing with our Father in Heaven. Whether we call it our "quiet time," "devotions," or something else, it is essential to our growth and fruitfulness.

Jesus Himself demonstrated the need for a "quiet time." Mark 1:21-34 records a long day in the life of Jesus. It was the Sabbath, and Jesus and His disciples went to the synagogue in Capernaum. Jesus taught there as one who had authority, and there He encountered a man with an unclean spirit from whom He cast out the demon. After leaving the synagogue, Jesus went into the house of Simon and Andrew. There He found Simon's mother-in-law ill, and He healed her. After dark, others were brought to Him. He healed them of various diseases and cast out many devils. After such a long and busy day, one might expect Jesus to "sleep in" the following morning. However, Mark 1:35 reports, "Very early in the morning, while it was still dark, Jesus got up, left the house and went off to a solitary place, where he prayed." Even after a stressful, tiring day, Jesus did not neglect to get up early for His "quiet time."

Make it a priority. If we choose to have a "quiet time" only when we can find time to do so, we will never build a strong relationship with the Lord. We must set the time aside. It should become as much a part of our daily schedules as eating breakfast or lunch. *When* we schedule it is not as important as making sure it is somewhere in our schedules. However, for many people, early in the day is best. It is good to spend some time with God before encountering the problems of the day. We don't necessarily need to set aside a large amount of time (even though that would be commendable), but it would be wise to start with at least fifteen minutes, jealously guarding that time each day.

Focus on the purpose. Our "quiet time" is not a time to search for information in the Bible. It is a time when we allow God to speak to us and when we speak to God. The "quiet time" is not for studying our Sunday School lesson or searching for a passage to which we can refer a friend in crisis. We need to let God speak to us through His Word.

Choose a method. The method may vary from time to time, but when we sit down for our "quiet time," we will gain the most from it when we include the following ingredients:

(1) Read the Word. Do not take large chunks but concentrate on a small section. A good place to start is with the Proverbs or one of the shorter epistles, taking a few verses each day.

(2) Meditate on the Word. In I Timothy 4:15 Paul wrote, "Be diligent in these matters; give yourself wholly to them, so that everyone may see your progress." Perhaps the word which best defines "meditation" is "digestion." We need to spend some time digesting what we have read.

(3) Decide how the Word applies to you. Ray Baughman in his book, *The Abundant Life*, suggests we ask such questions as: What commands are there in this passage for

me to obey? What sins are mentioned that I must give up? What promises are there for me to claim? What examples are there in this passage that I ought to follow? Remember to keep the "I" out front. Let God speak to *you*.

(4) Pray about the Word. Stop and talk with God about what is being placed in your heart as you read and meditate. When you read about the greatness of God, you will probably want to stop and praise Him. When you read of His love and how that love has been manifested, you will want to say, "Thank you." You will be reminded by Scripture of sin in your life of which you will want to repent. You will become aware of your weaknesses and will find yourself compelled to talk with God about them. As in any conversation, when God speaks to you, it will prompt you to talk with Him.

Don't neglect it. There is probably nothing more important to us than building a strong devotional life. It may be the single most important factor in our Christian growth. To neglect our "quiet time" is to place ourselves in a position of possible spiritual starvation. To make it a part of our daily schedules is to put ourselves into a position to receive and to give multiple blessings. Those who reach maximum fruitfulness are those who spend quality time with God.

PRINCIPLES TO PONDER:

1. Both impromptu and planned prayer are essential to a balanced prayer life.

2. Faith is the foundation of a successful prayer life.

3. Our prayer life is affected by how we view others, ourself, and the Lord.

4. Time with God at the beginning of the day will help insure a fruitful day.

5. A proper quiet time includes both speaking to God and allowing Him to speak to us.

6. Apart from God's power, we cannot bear any fruit.

PRACTICING THE PRINCIPLES:

1. List the six principles for correctly approaching God and rate on a scale of one to ten your success in practicing each of those principles. Draw up a definite plan to enable you to improve the three you rated lowest.

2. If you do not presently have a quiet time, get up fifteen minutes earlier each day for the next month, spending that extra time with God. At the end of that month, evaluate your need to continue this practice.

3. Using Matthew 6:5-18 as a reference, make a list of dos and don'ts for an effective devotional life. Ask a Christian friend to do the same and then compare the two lists and make the comparison the basis for a discussion.

chapter eleven

Choose the Right Accountability

Accountability becomes a definite factor early in life. Two-year-old Jimmy is reluctant to chase the ball into the street. Why? It's probably not so much his fear of approaching traffic as his knowledge that he will have to answer to Mom or Dad for his actions. When he is a little older, he does his school work and behaves himself relatively well in class. Is it because he is naturally a good child? Maybe, but another explanation is that he knows he must answer to his teacher day by day and his parents on report card day. He knows he can expect trouble when he falters and a pat on the back when he does what needs to be done.

After completing his formal education, Jimmy enters the job market, finding that not much has changed. His job comes with a whole network of checks and balances. About this time he may fall in love with the girl of his dreams and wedding bells bring still more accountability. It never ends.

The weight of accountability may seem like a burden. Its ever-lingering presence can create the feeling that freedom really does not exist. We may feel smothered by the constant demands to open the books on our lives for regular inspection. As children, we dreamed of the time when we would be on our own, not answering to anyone, but that dream goes unfulfilled. We always seem tangled in the web of accountability—but is that bad?

Some of life's grandest blessings are disguised as burdens. The weight of accountability is not wasted. It affords some splendid benefits for those striving for fruitfulness in a hostile world.

Why Accountability?

Common sense enables us to recognize at least five positive benefits of accountability.

We are motivated by accountability. "Why do people perform as expected?" a seminar leader asked.

The eager participants shot back several answers. Love, ambition, survival, and security were some of the factors mentioned.

"Those are good answers," our leader explained, "and they certainly play a part in motivating us, but the most prominent reason people do what is expected of them is 'accountability'—they know someone is checking on them."

I hated to admit it, but the more I thought about it, the more convinced I was that he was on target. Looking back over my life, I remembered many duties I had performed simply because someone had held me accountable. Not only that, but I have been known to abstain from questionable activities primarily because I feared the consequences of being found out.

That revelation does little for my ego, but it certainly helps me appreciate the fact that I am always in a position of accountability. We like to think we are self-motivated, doing all of the right things for the right reasons. Some people hate the idea of being answerable to anyone. But I know that I need all the help I can get to keep me doing the right things.

Our ideas are refined by accountability. Solomon wrote, "Plans fail for lack of counsel, but with many advisers they succeed" (Proverbs 15:22).

Ideas are conceived by individuals, but refined by a multiplicity of input. An idea left to one person rarely blooms to its full potential.

"I was more excited with my idea for reorganizing my department than any of my other brainstorms since becoming departmental supervisor," Jim said. "However, my boss didn't like it nearly as much as I did." Jim went on to explain, "He found flaws in my plan that I would never have caught in a million years. But it turned out all right," he declared with a smile. "Several of us worked on the concept for several weeks and eventually it was incorporated. Today it's working beautifully," he said with obvious pride.

Jim's unrefined plan undoubtedly would have flopped had he not been accountable to someone. Additional input helps us refine our ideas, see them from different perspectives. Accountability provides a sounding board and can help us benefit from sound advice.

We receive affirmation from accountability. When I expressed my appreciation to a member of my staff for a job well done, that staff member responded with a sigh of relief. "I needed to hear that!" she explained. "I wasn't sure I was moving in the right direction."

That staff person performed with much more confidence from that day on, and the fruit from her performance was encouraging. Accountability affords opportunity for reinforcement. Such affirmation encourages us to proceed with confidence.

Our vision is enlarged by accountability. Tunnel vision can be an obstacle to effective service. Left alone, one may cling to limited interests and narrow views, but accountability forces us to consider other viewpoints. Our world is enlarged by the necessity of answering to another.

I am not a gifted soul-winner. It is not my nature to be aggressive. In fact, a junior high teacher gave me a nickname, "the sphinx"—the silent stone face. I remember knocking on doors in the early months of my ministry while praying no one was home. It was sheer torture, but I talked with some about the Lord and some were saved. In those days I mustered up enough courage to visit in homes for one reason—it was expected of me! I knew the Lord expected it of me, and the leaders of my church expected it of me. Today, few duties delight me as much as sharing Christ with those I visit, but it took accountability to get me on the right road. My vision was enlarged because I was accountable to God and the leaders of my church.

We receive protection through accountability. I can think of two ways accountability provides protection. First, it gives us extra incentive to stand firm in the face of temptation. Temptation is not as attractive when we face the probability of exposure. Accountability increases the likelihood that someone will know about our moment of weakness, thus making the possibility of yielding less likely.

Second, a system of accountability decreases the likelihood that we will be falsely accused of sin we did not commit. Accountability provides witnesses to one's innocence.

Bill received that notice almost all of us fear will some day show up in our mailbox. It was signed by an I.R.S. representative, soliciting Bill's presence in his office on a specific day at a particular time. The purpose of the meeting? To conduct an audit of Bill's previous year's tax records.

Bill's friend, Ed, later inquired, "Are you intimidated by the prospects of such a session?"

Bill's answer is a classic. "I have nothing to hide," he said. "It's an opportunity to prove my honesty."

What a great attitude! Accountability is a terrific opportunity to confirm our integrity and thus make it possible for us to affirm our position of ambassadors for Christ and reach the highest level of usefulness for Him.

The Principle Of Credibility By Accountability

John Smith receives what he interprets as a call from the Lord to establish a para-church organization. He reasons that the Lord has called *him* to this important work, so the feasibility of sharing leadership with anyone is not considered. A board of directors is selected, but the directors are essentially "rubber stamps" for John Smith's ideas and programs. John Smith is accountable to no one but the Lord. He is the one and only undisputed leader of the organization.

The ministry grows rapidly. Thousands of people are blessed by the work. Many of them unselfishly want others to experience similar blessings, so they support John Smith's ministry with significant gifts.

John Smith is in the spotlight. As a nationally-known

personality, he becomes a target for random pot shots. Some critics accuse him of taking for personal use money donated to the ministry. Another questions his ministry decisions, while still others allege unethical actions by members of his staff.

The public is drawn quickly into the controversy. John Smith is guilty of none of the accusations, but without the protection that a system of accountability provides, he has difficulty proving his innocence. His only defense is his word, and that is not enough for the doubting public. Soon his ministry is only a shell of what it was once.

The principle of "credibility by accountability" simply stated is: *The more substantial the system of accountability, the greater the protection against false accusations and misunderstandings.* No other protection affords the advantage of having several people constantly looking over our shoulders.

"It sounds reasonable," you say, "but I will never head a para-church organization! How does this principle apply to me?" The principle is the same for anyone involved in any endeavor, church related or secular. Accountability is an invaluable aid in keeping our reputations above reproach, enabling us to continue serving the Lord and providing the premium fruit of righteousness for a skeptical world.

"You have convinced me," you say. "Accountability should be pursued rather than shunned, but where do I look for a legitimate system of accountability?"

Accountable To Whom?
Accountability is found by establishing a relationship with the Lord. Paul wrote to the Romans:

For none of us lives to himself alone and none
of us dies to himself alone. If we live, we live
to the Lord; and if we die, we die to the Lord.
So, whether we live or die, we belong to the Lord.
For this very reason, Christ died and returned
to life so that he might be the Lord of both the
dead and the living. You then, why do you judge
your brother? Or why do you look down on your
brother? For we will all stand before God's judgment
seat. It is written: "As surely as I live," says the
Lord, "every knee will bow before me; every
tongue will confess to God.

So then, each of us will give an account of
himself to God."

(14:7-12)

Four life-altering facts leap out of those verses.
(1) No Christian is an island, answerable only to self.
(2) We are accountable to the Lord in both life and death.
(3) We are accountable to the Lord for only our own
    actions.
(4) Eventually, everyone will acknowledge the supreme
    authority of Jesus.
What do these truths mean? For one thing, they suggest
it is appropriate for Christians to consider carefully the Lord's
will before every action. Paul described Christ as, "far above
all rule and authority, power and dominion, and every title
that can be given, not only in the present age but also
in the one to come." He goes on to state, "And God placed
all things under his feet and appointed him to be head over
everything for the church" (Ephesians 1:21-22).

Our society has built-in systems of accountability. The
system of government under which we live, the justice sys-

tem, and the pecking order of the place where we are employed are all examples of accountability imposed on us by such factors as residence and employment.

How are we to respond to such systems? Peter leaves no room for speculation on that question. His instructions are unquestionably clear.

> Submit yourselves for the Lord's sake to every authority instituted among men: whether to the king, as the supreme authority, or to governors, who are sent by him to punish those who do wrong and to commend those who do right. For it is God's will that by doing good you should silence the ignorant talk of foolish men. Live as free men, but do not use your freedom as a cover-up for evil; live as servants of God. Show proper respect to everyone: Love the brotherhood of believers, fear God, honor the king.
>
> (I Peter 2:13-17)

Humanity also provides a system of accountability. We call that system, "a family." In Ephesians 5:22—6:4 Paul deals with the relationship and accountability of wife to husband, husband to wife, and children to parents.

That section starts with instructions for wives: "Wives, submit to your husbands as to the Lord....Now as the church submits to Christ, so also wives should submit to their husbands in everything."

The accountability of the marriage relationship is not a one-sided proposition, though. Paul exhorts, "Husbands love your wives, just as Christ loved the church and gave himself up for her." Husbands are bound by the most binding accountability of all—the accountability of love!

The accountability aspect of the marriage relationship

is summarized in verse 33, "Each one of you also must love his wife as he loves himself, and the wife must respect her husband."

In the first two verses of the sixth chapter, instructions to sons and daughters are given, "Children, obey your parents in the Lord, for this is right. Honor your father and mother—which is the first commandment with a promise."

Still another means of obtaining greater accountability is to volunteer accountability to selected people—the accountability of friendship. A covenant of accountability with people we love and respect can be a wonderful blessing.

Once, out of frustration, I was publicly unkind to a friend. A few minutes later another friend, Earl, said to me rather forcefully, "You owe Virchil an apology." He was right, and I immediately gave that apology to Virchil, also publicly.

When Earl exposes my mistakes, I listen. I know he loves me and wants my ministry to succeed. Likewise, when he commends me, it means something, for he is refreshingly honest. My covenant of accountability with Earl is informal. No contract has been drawn up, but it is binding.

There is one other place to find accountability. *It seems certain one reason the Lord instituted the church was for spiritual accountability.*

Scripture instructs, "Obey your leaders and submit to their authority. They keep watch over you as men who must give an account. Obey them so that their work will be a joy, not a burden, for that would be of no advantage to you" (Hebrews 13:17).

Accountability provided by a congregation, however, goes beyond members submitting to church leaders. Paul wrote to the church at Ephesus, "Submit to one another out of reverence for Christ" (5:21).

Peter also directs Christians to be accountable to one

another: "Young men, in the same way be submissive to those who are older. All of you, clothe yourselves with humility toward one another, because, God opposes the proud but gives grace to the humble" (I Peter 5:5).

More than fifty passages in the New Testament encourage Christians to minister to "one another." It is not logical to believe one can be all God intends a person to be without having the advantage of mutual submission in the fellowship of a body of believers. We need the checks and balances that such a relationship furnishes. That is one reason every Christian needs to be an active participant with a local body of believers.

Breaking Down Resistance To Accountability

Several character traits strengthen our ability to accept and even solicit accountability.

Trust. Confidence in those to whom accountability is required enables us to feel good about answering to others. Accepting accountability can be difficult when one is prone to be untrusting. When that suspicious nature is conquered, accountability is less objectionable.

Self-Esteem. One may resist accountability because of a poor opinion of self. When we do not like the person we have become, we will not want to reveal that person to others. Learning to accept accountability is sometimes a matter of realizing each one of us is unique and special in our own way.

Humility. Accepting accountability requires us to acknowledge our inadequacies. One with a "know it all" attitude will not be willing to answer to anyone. What good can come from listening to someone else when we already know everything? Peter wrote: "Humble yourselves, therefore, under God's mighty hand, that he may lift you up in due time" (I Peter 5:6).

Patience. I remember the frustration in my early years of ministry with the time frame required to get decisions ratified in the local church. It seemed to take months to move from an idea to an "official decision." That is the way of accountability. It requires time and effort, and those who have mastered patience will find it easier to accept.

Perception. Solomon wrote, "...Fools despise wisdom and discipline" (Proverbs 1:7). The other side is that perceptive people walk in wisdom, practicing discipline. That includes the discipline of yielding to the evaluation of those who occupy positions of supervision over us—even if we're the ones who gave them that privilege. It all works together to enable us to achieve a higher degree of fruitfulness than would be possible without proper accountability.

PRINCIPLES TO PONDER:

1. A position of accountability is a positive position in which to be.

2. Accountability is as much for affirmation as correction.

3. Credibility is enhanced by accountability.

4. The building of relationships is valuable to obtaining proper accountability.

5. Ultimately, we are accountable to God.

6. The more secure we are, the more likely we will respond positively to accountability.

PRACTICING THE PRINCIPLES:

1. List all the people to whom you are accountable, attempting to determine if your network for accountability is sufficient.

2. Write a brief contract for a covenant of "friendship accountability," and then pray about entering into an agreement with a Christian friend.

3. Read the four chapters of the book of Philippians, searching for hints as to whom Paul considered himself accountable.

chapter twelve

Choose the Right Approach

"Rome wasn't built in a day," my high school track coach reminded me when I showed disappointment at my first timing in the two-mile event. "Work hard and take it one day at a time. You'll get better," he assured me.

I did, and later found that it is also good advice for anyone who has a burning desire to be a successful servant of the Lord. It is easy to become frustrated when we start comparing ourselves to *Super Christian*. When we foul up, we may wonder, "Will I ever measure up?" For those caught up in the myth of perfection, my advice is: Work hard and take one day at a time.

While living in Indiana, I saw lots of tall corn, but I never observed it growing. Even the fastest growing crop does not grow rapidly enough to allow us to actually see the growth take place. (Despite the claims of some farmers I know!) Progress is usually gradual, often imperceptible.

There will be times when we will not measure up even to our own expectations. We will stumble along the way. We should be disappointed at our failures—but never discouraged by them. Those who grow the most delicious fruit are those who get up from their failure, use its lessons as steppingstones, and plow ahead with even greater determination than before, having grown stronger from that failure.

Someone said, "We have met the enemy and he is us." That can be true of Christians, too. We can become the most prohibitive obstacle to our own progress. It can happen when we refuse to forget the past or when we insist upon worrying about tomorrow.

However, we don't have to be hindered from fruitful living by our own anxiety. We don't have to get down on ourselves. We can *work hard and take it one day at a time*. As long as we are learning, trying, we are bound to get better.

We will also accomplish the most when we manage to stay encouraged. We are more likely to stay encouraged when we approach life with the right attitude about the past, present, and future. Keeping yesterday, today, and tomorrow in the proper perspective is the key.

Yesterday Doesn't Have To Hinder

When I was in high school, a friend of mine introduced me to his great uncle. He later told me the old gentleman had spent much of his life crippled by one bad decision.

Many years before, he had been offered an opportunity to invest in a relatively new company. After giving due consideration to the proposal, he decided to pass, feeling it would be an unwise investment. That company was the Coca-Cola Bottling Company. The investment opportunity he passed up would have netted him millions and given him security for a lifetime. My friend said his great uncle never recovered from that lost opportunity. He spent much of his life hampered by his grief and regret over what could have been.

Fretting over past mistakes which have already been forgiven by God is a sure way to limit the future. Paul had some things in his past which were undoubtedly grief-filled memories. He'd consented to the stoning of Stephen and hauled Christians off to dungeons, torture, and death (Acts 7:60—8:3).

When he wrote to the Philippians, he told them, "Forgetting what is behind and straining toward what is ahead, I press on..." (3:13-14). Later, in chapter 4, verses 6 and 7, he added, "Do not be anxious about anything, but in everything...present your requests to God. And the peace of God...will guard your hearts and minds in Christ Jesus." The psalmist also declared a comforting truth when he said, "As far as the east is from the west, so far has he removed our transgressions from us" (Psalm 103:12). Mistakes, regrets, lost opportunities touch every life, but they don't have to cripple you forever.

Jimmy made some mistakes that scarred his life terribly. Those mistakes led to a divorce from his wife of several years. He started drinking in an effort to escape his troubles. The drinking just led to more problems. Jimmy came to me for counseling several times. In one such session I told him, "You must understand that God is willing to forgive you."

With tears swelling up in his eyes he answered, "I know

God is willing to forgive me, but I am not sure *I* am willing to forgive me."

Being a staunch baseball fan, I know every major league baseball team plays one hundred and sixty-two games in the course of a season. No team has ever won all their games. In fact, no team has ever won as many as one hundred and thirty of those games. However, the players on top notch baseball teams go out to win every ballgame. They know they will lose some, but they still go out to win every game. When they do lose, they shake it off and go out on the diamond the next day just as determined as the day before, perhaps even more so.

We cannot "win them all" in the game of life either, but it is good to approach life expecting to do so. When we do lose one, we need to get up and face the next day with even more determination. We need to learn how to shake off our failures and move on to victory.

"Yesterday" does not have to be a millstone around our necks. It can be a foundation upon which to build.

When I began my ministry in Shelbyville, Indiana, the building was literally "everywhere." The four-month-old sanctuary had collapsed under the weight of ice and snow. No doubt some mistakes had been made in either design or construction or, perhaps, both. We tried to learn from those mistakes, making some major alterations when we rebuilt. But it is rather interesting that we constructed the second building right on top of the slab on which the first sanctuary sat. There was something left from the failure on which to rebuild a more secure structure.

Even when we fail, something good may grow from the failure. Fruitfulness is greatly enhanced by learning to build on failures. The difference between fruitfulness and stagnation is often in how we handle yesterday's mistakes.

I once confessed a rather serious mistake to one of my colleagues, expecting him to scold me. But with an understanding smile and from a sympathetic heart he responded by simply asking, "What did you learn from your mistake?" What we learn from yesterday's mistake may become the vehicle that will usher in tomorrow's victory.

We can also build on yesterday's successes. Why have scientists accomplished more in the last fifty years than all the scientists before them combined? It is probably because scientists of today have all the foundational discoveries of the past on which to build. They did not have to start from scratch. Nor do we have to start from scratch each day. We can build on all we have learned and experienced in the past...and even from mistakes we see in others' lives.

We can serve today and in the future with greater results because of yesterday. Yesterday can be one of our most valuable assets when its fruits are used correctly. That should be true regardless of whether the past has been glorious, disastrous, or, as in most cases, a combination of the two. Yesterday has given us some valuable experiences we would be foolish to ignore.

Today Is For Living

Jesus said, "Therefore do not worry about tomorrow, for tomorrow will worry about itself" (Matthew 6:34). That's true! It is the present that requires our very best effort.

Escapism is never the answer, either. Who can forget Scarlet O'Hara's recurring line in Margaret Mitchell's *Gone With the Wind*, "I'll think about that tomorrow?" Life is often approached with the Scarlet O'Hara philosophy and when it is, the result may be alcoholism, drug addiction, obesity, TV addiction, promiscuity, or some other serious problem. Such extremities are often the result of the need to escape. When we refuse to deal with today, tomorrow isn't likely to be any better. The best way to improve tomorrow is to give our best effort today.

"I'm going to get my act together eventually," a young lady told me, but a great deal of time has elapsed and, as far as I know, she has made very few alterations. If we wait for "eventually" to happen, the final curtain may fall before our act even makes it to the stage.

Procrastination has a crippling effect. There is a vast potential for disastrous problems when one insists upon putting off until tomorrow what should have been done today. There are some real dangers in that approach.

If or when the task is finally done, it will likely be more difficult than it would have been if given the proper attention earlier. A friend is always going on a diet *tomorrow.* Tomorrow never comes and he keeps getting heavier. If he ever does get around to that diet, he will have much more weight to lose than several years ago when he first started talking about a diet. His task has become larger and harder because of procrastination.

That is the idea behind Paul's command, "Do not let the sun go down while you are still angry, and do not give the devil a foothold" (Ephesians 4:26-27). If we're angry with someone, it is best for us to go immediately to that person and attempt to work things out before it balloons into a larger task. When we put off dealing with the problem, we allow it to smolder and to blow up out of proportion. That gives the devil a foothold. Problems we do not deal with just get worse and jobs left undone become larger.

Procrastination leaves us less time to complete the task. With each day that passes, we are one day closer to that unknown time when this life will end. "I have plenty of time" is not a valid statement because we cannot be sure of another hour or even another minute. It's also true that there are some endeavors that will never be completed. We will never know and understand all of God's Word. We will never lead every person in the world to the Lord. We will never develop the perfect relationship with the Lord. But the sooner we get started, the more time we will have for the task. More time will enable us to get closer than we otherwise would be and do more good. The Lord has given us some pretty big responsibilities, so the best approach is simply to get on with it. Jesus told His disciples, "As long as it is day, we must do the work of Him who sent me. Night is coming, when no one can work" (John 9:4).

James wrote of the uncertainty beyond today. "Now listen, you who say, 'Today or tomorrow we will go to this or that city, spend a year there, carry on business and make money.' Why, you do not even know what will happen tomorrow. What is your life? You are a mist that appears for a little while and then vanishes...Anyone, then, who knows the good he ought to do and doesn't do it, sins" (4:13-14,17).

Everything beyond today is bonus time.

Procrastination robs us of blessings. Every day we put off doing that to which God has called us is another day of blessing we miss. Every day we put off seriously investing our lives for the Lord is another day without successes that could have been ours. "I am enjoying this so much," a lady told me after her two week involvement in a Bible study. "I don't know why I didn't get started a long time ago."

Procrastination robs the Lord's work of victories. There

are some opportunities available to us today which will not be there tomorrow. If we are not willing to take advantage of those opportunities today, they will be lost forever.

Many years ago, Roy Gustafson wrote in *Decision* an account of a tourist who visited an exquisite garden on one of the large estates in Italy.

The tourist struck up a conversation with the caretaker.

"How long have you been here?" he asked.

"Twenty-five years," came the answer.

"And how often has the owner been to see the estate in those twenty-five years?" he probed.

"Four times," the caretaker responded.

"When did he come last?"

The caretaker patiently answered, "Twelve years ago."

"Does he ever write to you?"

"He never writes me. I get my orders from the steward in Milan," the old man explained.

The tourist was amazed. "You are here pretty much on your own, yet you keep the garden so spick-and-span that one would think you were expecting the owner tomorrow."

"Today, sir, today!" came the answer.[1]

We accomplish the most when we live each day as if we will have to stand before our Lord at the end of today and give account.

Tomorrow Can Be Faced With Confidence

Many of our worries are borrowed from tomorrow. We can face the future with more confidence when we practice two principles.

First, recognize that tomorrow's task is not usually as overwhelming as our fears anticipate. I learned that years ago when I was invited to speak in the chapel service of a prestigious Bible college and seminar. After accepting the invitation, I immediately started thinking about the task before me. I was only twenty-nine-years old, and, at that time, I had done absolutely no graduate study. I would speak to young men who, in some cases, had more education than I. Some of the professors who would be present were recognized scholars.

I worked myself into a fit of anxiety in anticipation of that chapel service. I drove the hundred miles that morning in fear and trembling. I considered the possibility that I might get caught in traffic and not make it to the school in time to preach, finding some comfort in that thought. When it became obvious that the traffic would not be a factor, another thought ran through my mind, "If I am lucky, I'll have an accident that will prevent me from going through with this."

There was no accident and when I got there, I found everyone to be very gracious and responsive. I enjoyed myself enormously. My reaction to the morning was positive. "That wasn't bad," I said to myself as I drove home. "I hope they invite me back sometime." I did all that worrying for no reason and let it rob my days of joy. We can find strength for the future in the fact that most things turn out to be not as bad as we thought they were going to be.

Second, we can face tomorrow's task with confidence when we realize we will have greater strength for tomorrow than we have today. That is the beautiful thing about spiritual growth. There is always more strength for tomorrow.

Scripture says, "Your strength will equal your days. There is no one like the God of Jeshurun, who rides on the heavens to help you" (Deuteronomy 33:25-26).

When I was a child, I foolishly worried about someday performing the everyday functions of an adult. I didn't see how I could ever do such things as drive a car. The mistake, of course, was that I matched my anticipated future activities with my present abilities. As an eight-year-old, driving a car was beyond my range of capability, but as a sixteen-year-old, I was capable of handling it. Our abilities will increase as the days pass.

We don't have to fall into a state of anxiety over fear of tomorrow. Tomorrow we will be better equipped to handle whatever the Lord allows to come our way. Take one day at a time is some of the best advice I ever received or, in the words of Scripture, "Do not worry about tomorrow, for tomorrow will worry about itself. Each day has enough trouble of its own" (Matthew 6:34).

FOOTNOTE

[1]Taken from *Decision* magazine, October, 1962; © 1962 Billy Graham Evangelistic Association. Used by permission. All rights reserved.

PRINCIPLES TO PONDER:

1. The right approach to accomplishing the most in life is to work hard and take one day at a time.

2. There is often something left from past mistakes upon which something solid can be built.

3. Today's responsibilities are best dealt with today.

4. Tomorrow can be faced with confidence by keeping both the difficulties of the future task and the strength of our future ability in godly perspective.

5. Action, not time, solves problems.

PRACTICING THE PRINCIPLES:

1. Recall a failure experienced more than three years back and then list every lesson and benefit that came to you as a result of that failure. Take some time to thank God for using a bad time in your life for good.

2. Making a list of everything you have been putting off, start today systematically completing those jobs.

3. Read Hebrews 13:8, jotting down the implications of that verse of Scripture.

chapter thirteen

Choose the Right Harvest

The young man sitting in my study was agonizing over a series of business and family decisions that had backfired on him. There was a moment of silence as he slumped low in his chair. Then looking away from me he mumbled, "Decisions are hard."

We have seen that making the right choice can be complicated. And, like the young man in my office, we all have made some poor choices. The problem with choices is that there is more than one option open to us. That, after all, is what makes them choices.

Constantly having to choose from two or more options available to us can become burdensome, but it is a burden for which we can be thankful. God gave us a mind, a will, and the ability to reason. Perhaps life would be easier if

God had created us as some kind of spiritual robots whose every step is determined by the Master Controller in Heaven. At times, we may feel it would be nice to by-pass the process of trying to determine God's will in every matter. However, to lose that God-given freedom of choice would be to lose the blessing of a special relationship with God which is ours by virtue of being in His image (Genesis 1:27). God expects us to make choices, right choices that plant, nurture and harvest the fruit of righteousness in us.

In Ephesians 5:8-11, Paul reminds us that we choose either fruitfulness or unfruitfulness. He exhorts: "Live as children of light (for the fruit of the light consists in all goodness, righteousness and truth) and find out what pleases the Lord. Have nothing to do with the fruitless deeds of darkness."

The fruit of righteousness is the goodness, right actions, and truth in our lives that produce the God-honoring triumphs that come out of a heart that is set on pleasing the Lord. Such fruit is the result of choosing righteous living and commitment to the sovereignty of Christ in our lives. A positive, willing response to the Holy Spirit who lives in us is also required (Galatians 5:22-23) for well-rounded fruit.

In the parable of the vine and branches, Jesus said, "I am the true vine, and my Father is the gardener" (John 15:2). When we understand that God is the gardener, we have a better grasp of what Jesus meant when He said, "This is to my Father's glory, that you bear much fruit, showing yourselves to be my disciples" (John 15:8).

Quality and quantity. Our fruit reflects on the ability of the One doing the planting and tending.

We strive to grow the fruit of righteousness in order

to call attention to God, who is the source of the good
fruit we bear.

Know Where You Are Going

Perhaps you remember, from the story *Alice in Wonderland*, the question Alice asked of the Cheshire Cat.
"Would you tell me, please," she said, "which way I ought
to walk from here?"

The Cat replied, "That depends a good deal on where
you want to get to."

Alice said, "I don't much care where."

"Then," said the Cat, "it doesn't matter which way you
walk."

Making choices that produce the fruit of righteousness
requires a one-way mindset. They begin with a definite
idea of where we want to go. The wise Christian does not
lose sight of his or her reason for living because choices
are most difficult when one is undecided about destination.

Joshua called upon the people of Israel to make the choice
that would determine the direction of their lives and allow
them to make the everyday choices with which they would
be confronted. He demanded: "Now fear the Lord and serve
him with all faithfulness....But if serving the Lord seems
undesirable to you, then choose for yourselves this day whom
you will serve....But as for me and my household, we will
serve the Lord" (Joshua 24:14-15).

Joshua's message is simple: "You need to choose *today*;
you need to choose *for yourself*, and you need to choose
God." When such a commitment is made, the direction
for our lives is determined, and the options open to us
have narrowed considerably.

To choose God is to choose His way, His work, and

His Word. We are obligated to make decisions that will enable us to be faithful servants to Him.

One of the great challenges for a Christian is the challenge to stay on track, to remain focused on the way we have chosen. Making that choice to serve the Lord without compromise is wonderful because we have a purpose which makes choices easier than if we were floundering about with no commanding direction or purpose.

Make Complete Choices

As this study about making right choices in growing the fruit of righteousness comes to an end, let's look at the final three steps necessary.

(1) A choice starts with an *intellectual* decision. One examines all the facts and decides which is the proper direction. Such discernment is easy in some cases, but in others, an intense effort may be required in order to come to the right conclusions. To go through life using the coin-flipping method would be perilous. Right choices are made by those who commit themselves to searching out and carefully weighing the facts.

(2) A choice includes an *emotional* decision. Even when one has concluded that the facts clearly point in a particular direction, the choice has not yet been made. We have not chosen until we have decided with both mind and heart that it is the way to go. The choice is not completed until we are convinced that we *want* to move in that direction. We go through life with our chins high and our backs straight when we have confidence that we are going where we are supposed to go and doing what is right for us to do.

(3) A choice is not completed until the decision has been *acted upon.* We can know in our minds and hearts what

is right and still refuse or neglect to take the right action. This is like a little boy confronted by his mother after it became obvious he had neglected a chore she had explicitly instructed him to do. He defended himself with this argument: "My mind told me what I was supposed to do, but my feet didn't listen."

A choice has been made when we decide with mind and heart what we are to do and then do it. It is when we have finally acted on our convictions that a choice has actually been made. The challenge is that when the three-part process of choosing is completed, the result will be a magnificent harvest of fruit that glorifies the Lord.

Choose Well

We live in a "wrong-way" world, a world ruled by Satan, the prince of this world (Ephesians 2:1-3). Making God-honoring choices in such an environment can never be easy, but it can be done. Paul gave these instructions to the Romans—and to us: "Do not conform any longer to the pattern of this world, but be transformed by the renewing of your mind. Then you will be able to test and approve what God's will is—his good, pleasing and perfect will" (12:2).

Freedom to choose is one of God's greatest blessings, but with the blessing comes the burden of responsibility and accountability. To make choices is easy, to make *right* choices is often hard.

At a church picnic, two captains chose their teams for a friendly game of touch football. After his team came away with a convincing, one-sided victory, the captain of the winning team, a bit disappointed with his own play declared, "But I chose well." Indeed he did, and when life is over, I hope we will be able to look back and say the same thing.

Making good choices is vital in the process of growing the choicest fruit of righteousness in our lives. Good choices are essential to our ability to lift up Christ before a world gone wrong. Choose well! Your fruitfulness depends on it.